WAGNER

WAGNER
from a drawing by Middlehurst

WAGNER

by W. J. TURNER

GREENWOOD PRESS, PUBLISHERS
WESTPORT, CONNECTICUT

Library of Congress Cataloging in Publication Data

Turner, Walter James, 1889-1946.
    Wagner.

    Reprint of the 1948 ed. published by A. A. Wyn,
New York.
    1. Wagner, Richard, 1813-1883. 2. Composers--
Germany--Biography.
ML410.W1T8 1979   782.1'092'4 [B]   78-12226
ISBN 0-313-21084-5

Originally published by A. A. Wyn, Inc., New York, N.Y.

Reprinted in 1979 by Greenwood Press, Inc.,
51 Riverside Avenue, Westport, CT 06880

Printed in the United States of America

10 9 8 7 6 5 4 3 2 1

CONTENTS

5

6 CONTENTS

CHRONOLOGY

1813 . . . . Wagner born on May 22nd at Leipzig, Saxony.

1822 . . . . Wagner attends Kreuzschule.

1827 . . . . Wagner enters Nicolaischule.

1830 . . . . Wagner attends Thomasschule. His overture in B flat performed under H. Dorn at the Leipzig Theatre.

1831 . . . . Matriculates at Leipzig University, February 23rd and becomes a pupil of Weinlig for composition.

1833 . . . . Chorus-master at Würzburg.

1834 . . . . Music-director at the Magdeburg Theatre.

1836 . . . . Married Minna Planer at Königsberg.

1837 . . . . Music-director at Riga.

1839 . . . . Leaves Riga for Paris via London.

1842 . . . . *Rienzi* produced at Dresden and Wagner made Court Conductor.

1849 . . . . Revolution in Dresden; Wagner flees to Switzerland.

1855 . . . . Visits London to conduct the Royal Philharmonic Society.

1861 . . . . Hears *Lohengrin* for the first time at Vienna.

1864 . . . . Naturalised as a Bavarian, and settles in Munich.

1870 . . . . Marries Cosima von Bülow (*née* Liszt).

1872 . . . . Settles at Bayreuth.

1876 . . . . The "Ring des Nibelungen" performed at Bayreuth.

1877 . . . . Visits London for the third time.

1882 . . . . First performance of *Parsifal* at Bayreuth.

1883 . . . . Dies at Venice, February 13th.

FIRST PERFORMANCES OF WAGNER
OPERAS

DATE	OPERA	PLACE
1836	*Das Liebesverbot*	Magdeburg
1842	*Rienzi*	Dresden
1843	*Der Fliegende Holländer* .	Dresden
1844	*Tannhäuser* . . .	Dresden
1850	*Lohengrin*	Weimar
1868	*Die Meistersinger* . .	Bayreuth
1876	*Der Ring des Nibelungen* (complete, including *Das Rheingold, Die Walküre, Siegfried* and *Götterdämmerung*) .	Bayreuth
1882	*Parsifal*	Bayreuth

POSTHUMOUSLY

1888	*Die Feen*	Munich

UNPERFORMED

—	*Die Hochzeit* . . .	—

8

CHAPTER I

1813–1834

Doubtful parentage – early interest in dramatic literature – first lessons in harmony – early attempts at composition – pianoforte and violin lessons – influence of the theatre and opera house – Goethe and Beethoven – lessons with Weinlig – early compositions – favourable conditions in Wagner's youth – first engagement as chorus-master – early operas – his physical and mental characteristics.

WAGNER was born on May 22nd, 1813, at Leipzig, where his reputed father, Friedrich Wagner, was a clerk in the police service. Friedrich Wagner died on November 22nd, six months after Wagner was born, and in August in the following year, 1814, his mother married a friend of her first husband, the actor Ludwig Geyer, by whom she had a daughter, Cäcilie, who was born on February 26th, six and a half months after her second marriage.

Geyer was an actor, and shortly after his marriage with Wagner's mother he received a permanent appointment at the Court Theatre, Dresden, where the family moved. Wagner was sent to school, and until he was fourteen years old he was known as Richard Geyer. There is some doubt as to whether Geyer was his real father or not, and it cannot be said that there is definite proof one way or the other. What has given plausibility to the suggestion is the fact that Wagner himself seems to have thought it possible or even probable, and his mind was so much occupied with the idea in 1869, when he was

9

writing his autobiography, that he seems to have
mentioned it to Nietzsche, and in a letter to
Nietzsche dated December 19th, 1869, he sends
him a crest and on January 16th, 1870, writes:

"The crest has turned out very well and we
have every reason to be grateful to you for the
careful attention you have given to the matter.
But just here again my old objection to the vulture
has forced itself on me; the vulture will certainly
be taken by everyone, at first sight, for an eagle
– for there is a monk-vulture that closely resembles
the eagle. But, as it is essential – on account of
the reference (or association) – that the vulture
shall be recognised definitely and at once, we beg
you to get the engraver, with the help of the best
picture obtainable of such an animal, to hang the
characteristic vulture ruff round the neck of the
bird. To be sure, this cannot be done without a
slight transformation of the neck; but no doubt
it will be all right."

This crest was printed on the title page of the
privately printed edition of Wagner's autobiography, *Mein Leben*, and the whole point of
Wagner's care that the bird should look like a
vulture and not like an eagle is that the world
geyer, or *geier*, which was his stepfather's name,
means in German *vulture*. There is no other
evidence that Geyer was his father – but there is
a certain amount of evidence against it. In the
first place it is odd that, after being called Richard
Geyer up to the age of fourteen, his name, pre-
sumably at the instigation of his mother, should
have been changed to Wagner – some years after
his stepfather's death. Secondly, although Geyer
was an actor and Friedrich Wagner a police

official, we can find no evidence of heredity through Geyer of Wagner's dramatic talent, because Wagner's elder brother, Carl Albert, who was indisputably the son of Friedrich Wagner, became a well-known actor and singer and finally stage-manager at Berlin and the father of a well-known singer, Johanna Jachmann-Wagner. Also two of Wagner's elder sisters, who also are indisputably Friedrich Wagner's children, namely, Johanna Rosalie and Clara Wilhelmine, became well known, the former as an actress, the latter as a singer.

The controversy about Wagner's parentage has been enlivened by the suggestion that Geyer was a Jewish name, and some racial theorists have pretended to find Jewish characteristics in Wagner's music and in his anti-semitism. But we are informed by Bournot, who wrote a book on Geyer, that he traced Geyer's family back to 1700, and throughout that period the Geyers were all of evangelical faith and had married Germans. Therefore, even if Geyer were Wagner's father, the amount of Jewish blood in Wagner can be extremely small, though it might be none the less potent.

Wagner was sent to the Dresden Kreuzschule, a classical school, where at the age of thirteen he translated the first three books of the Odyssey from the Greek to the German out of school hours. At the age of fifteen he was sent to the Nicholaischule at Leipzig, where the family had removed when his elder sister, Rosalie, had got a theatrical engagement there. He spent most of his time reading translations of Greek and Shakespearian dramas and writing tragedies in imitation of them. Wagner's knowledge of music was at that time almost non-existent. Praeger tells us that as a boy Wagner played always in a rough and ready way by ear. At the age of twelve he had a few pianoforte lessons, and in Leipzig the famous Gewandhaus orchestral concerts introduced him to the music of Beethoven, and he began to think of composing instead of writing dramas. He bought Logier's *Thorough-Bass* and studied it, and at the age of sixteen began to take lessons in harmony from G. Müller, a musician belonging to the Leipzig orchestra. Of these lessons he writes in *Mein Leben*:

"His teaching and exercises soon filled me with the greatest disgust, as to my mind it all seemed so dry. For me music was a spirit, a noble and mystic monster, and any attempt to regulate it seemed to lower it in my eyes. I gathered much more congenial instruction about it from Hoffmann's *Phantasiestücken* than from my Leipzig orchestra player."

Through the writers Hoffmann and Tieck, Wagner became acquainted at this early age with the stories of the "Minnesinger" and "Tannhäuser," and after hearing Beethoven's Pastoral Symphony he began to write a pastoral play, and he says:

"I had worked it out in what I felt sure must be an entirely unprecedented way. I chose Goethe's *Laune der Verliebten* as a model for the form and plot of my work. I scarcely even drafted out the libretto, however, but worked it out at the same time as the music and orchestration; so that while I was writing out one page of the score, I had not even thought out the words for the next page. I remember distinctly that, following this extraordinary method, although I had not acquired the slightest knowledge about writing for instruments, I actually worked out a fairly long passage which finally resolved itself into a scene for three female voices followed by the air for tenor. My bent for writing for orchestra was so strong that I procured a score of *Don Juan* and set to work on what I then considered a very careful orchestration of a fairly long air for soprano. I also wrote a quartet in D major after I had myself sufficiently mastered the alto for the viola, my ignorance of which had caused me great difficulty only a short time before, when studying a quartet by Haydn."

It was found that Wagner had not attended his school for six months, and a family council was held, at which, he says, he laid stress upon his bent for music. The family had the common idea that anyone who wanted to become a musician ought at least to learn to play one instrument thoroughly and proposed to send him to the famous pianist, Hummel; but Wagner protested that by "music" he meant composing, and, although in the course of time he picked up a way of playing on the pianoforte, he never became even a moderately good pianist, and the only other instrument he had any practical knowledge of was the violin. What this amounted to may be judged by his own observations:

"My mother, indeed, paid the violinist, Sipp (who was still playing in the Leipzig orchestra in 1865), eight thalers for a violin (I don't know what became of it), with which for three months I must have inflicted unutterable torture upon my mother and sister by practising in my tiny little room. I got so far as to play certain Variations in F sharp by Mayseder, but only reached the second or third. After that I have no further recollection of practising. . . ."

Although Wagner could never have earned a living by playing, except in the street as an itinerant musician, he is not the most extreme example of a musician of genius without capacity for more than a rough and ready way of performing on any musical instrument. Berlioz was even less competent, and Praeger relates how Wagner, if criticised on account of his clumsy fingering, would reply with characteristic waggishness: "I play a great deal better than Berlioz."

But one must not imagine that Wagner was quite incapable at the pianoforte; although he lacked technical accuracy and a professional method, he could make himself understood. He could always play his own compositions – though imperfectly – in a manner to astonish and move his hearers. Praeger relates that, when Wagner called on Meyerbeer in 1839 at Boulogne, on his way to Paris, he showed him the two acts he had composed of *Rienzi*:

"Wagner took his place at the piano without being asked and impetuously attacked the score in his own rough and ready manner. Meyerbeer was astonished at the rough handling of the piano. He was himself a highly finished performer on the instrument, having begun his artistic career as a pianist. Wagner supplied as well as he could the vocal parts (with as little technical perfection as his piano playing), whilst Meyerbeer carefully studied the score over the performer's shoulder. . . ."

Wagner picked up his musical training here
and there by instinct. He matriculated at the
University of Leipzig in 1831, but his chief educa-
tion may be said to have been got from the
Dresden Court Theatre and the Dresden Opera
House. Those who do not understand the cultural
importance of such institutions when efficiently
managed may be impressed by Wagner's own
words in *Mein Leben*:

"What in my childhood had been merely the
interest aroused by . . . curiosity now became a
more deep-seated and conscious passion. *Julius
Cæsar, Macbeth, Hamlet,* the plays of Schiller, and
to crown all, Goethe's *Faust,* excited and stirred
me deeply. The Opera was giving the first performances of Marshner's *Vampir* and *Templer und
Jüdin.* The Italian company arrived from Dresden
and fascinated the Leipzig audience by the con-
summate mastery of their art . . . another miracle
– which also came to us from Dresden – suddenly
gave a new direction to my artistic feelings and
exercised a decisive influence over my whole life.
This consisted of a special performance given by
Wilhelmine Schröder-Devrient, who at that time
was at the zenith of her artistic career, young,
beautiful and ardent, and whose like I have never
again seen on the stage. She made her appearance in *Fidelio.*[1]

"If I look back on my life as a whole, I can
find no event that produced so profound an
impression upon me."

This performance of Beethoven's *Fidelio,* like the
earlier experiences of his orchestral music, was
decisive in revealing to Wagner his own desires. He

[1] At Leipzig in 1832.

says: "After the performance I rushed to a friend's house and wrote a short note to the singer, in which I briefly told her that from that moment my life had acquired its true significance and that if in days to come she should ever hear my name praised in the world of art, she must remember she had that evening made me what I then swore it was my destiny to become. This note I left at her hotel and ran out into the night as if I were mad."

After matriculation at the University of Leipzig he became, for about six months, a pupil of Theodore Weinlig, the cantor at the Thomasschule and a sound musician. From Wagner's account of his instruction from Weinlig in *Mein Leben* it is clear that he learned a great deal from him. Weinlig won his sympathy, the master and pupil composed fugues in common:

"This common task of fugue writing," says Wagner, "established between me and my good-natured teacher the tenderest of ties, for from that moment we both enjoyed the lessons. I was astonished how quickly the time flew. In eight weeks I had not only gone through a number of the most intricate fugues, but had also waded through all kinds of difficult evolutions in counterpoint, when, one day, on bringing him an extremely elaborate double fugue, he took my breath away by telling me that after this there was nothing left for him to teach me.

"As I was not aware of any great effort on my part, I often wondered whether I had really become a well-equipped musician. Weinlig himself did not seem to attach much importance to what he taught me: he said, 'probably you will never

write fugues or canons; but what you have
mastered is independence: you can now stand
alone and rely upon having a fine technique at
your fingers' ends if you should want it.' "

One may feel inclined to doubt Wagner's
account of his degree of progress under Weinlig,
but nevertheless the fact that he was learning to
write music as one learns to write prose is clear
from the actual works which he composed about
this time, namely: a sonata in four movements
in B, Op. 1, and a polonaise for four hands in D,
Op. 2, which were both published by Breitkopf
and Härtel in 1832 through Weinlig's influence.
In addition to these he composed between 1831
and 1832 the following:

Fantasia in F minor for pianoforte,
    unpublished;
Overture in D minor, performed at the
    Leipzig Gewandhaus, February 23rd,
    1832, unpublished;
Overture to Raupach's drama *König Enzio*,
    performed in the Royal Theatre, Leipzig,
    March 16th, 1832, published by Breitkopf,
    1907;
Overture in C, performed at a Euterpe con-
    cert at Leipzig and at the Gewandhaus,
    April 30th, 1832, unpublished;
Overture *Polonia*, written at Leipzig, 1832
    (or possibly at Riga in 1836?), published,
    1904;
Symphony in C, performed at Prague,
    summer 1832; at the Euterpe, December
    1832; at the Gewandhaus, January 10th,
    1833.

B

It may seem surprising that an unknown youth of nineteen should have succeeded in getting all these early compositions performed immediately, but it is exactly here that we discover some of the advantages of the widespread musical culture in German-speaking countries and of the decentralisation of social and political life at the time. The number of German towns of all sizes – the smallest possessing at least a state, city or court theatre, to which dramatic and operatic companies came regularly from the larger centres – where there was an active musical and social life centring round the court of some prince, duke or king, and a sufficient nucleus of musicians to form an orchestra, offered the maximum of opportunity to young musicians and composers. Expenses were cheap and it cost next to nothing to perform new works. Conditions are much less favourable to-day, even in Germany, where there is still considerable decentralisation. In other countries, such as England, where almost all artistic activity is concentrated in our metropolis, the enormous rise in expenses and possible profits through catering professionally for public entertainment, when the public available numbers millions, excludes all possibility of artistic experiment that does not offer correspondingly enormous gains. There is no place for performance of immature operas or dramas by young writers who are feeling their way; and there is still less room for their possible later masterpieces, because there has been no period of development of artist and public together through experiment. Under the present conditions, in a city like London, for example, there is only the commerce of entertainment, that is, the business of making money by catering for public entertainment. This is "business" on a big scale, and it has no use or place for creative genius.

In Wagner's birthplace and at his time conditions were quite different, fortunately for him; and the performances of these early compositions must have been very stimulating. It was also possible to get work as a professional musician, and it was in 1833, at the age of twenty, that Wagner got his first professional engagement through his elder brother Albert. This brother was engaged at the Würzburg theatre as actor, singer and stage-manager, and he obtained for Wagner the post of chorus-master. Then he wrote the words and the music of his second opera, *Die Feen* (his first opera, *Die Hochzeit*, composed in 1832, is only a fragment of thirty-six pages). Wagner confesses that he felt quite an amateur as choir-master and that he was doing a thing which he "had no right to undertake"; but he was not the first nor the last young man of talent who has had to learn the job he was paid for doing while doing it.

He returned to Leipzig in 1834 with the score of *Die Feen* and attempted to get Ringelhardt, the director of the theatre, to perform it. He accepted it but did not do anything more, and *Die Feen* was first publicly produced more than fifty years later, at Munich, in 1888. In Leipzig, Wagner once again heard Wilhelmine Schröder-Devrient. Ten years later she was to be the principal singer, and Wagner the conductor, at the Dresden Opera House, and from 1842 to 1848 the two were in close contact. There can be no doubt that he learned a great deal from her. In 1834, however, he was only twenty-one years old and unknown. The operas of Bellini and Auber were at that time most popular; influenced by them, he started on a third opera, *Das Liebesverbot*, in which he abandoned his earlier models Beethoven and Weber; he even went so far in enthusiasm, produced by Schröder-Devrient's performance as Romeo in Bellini's opera, *Montecchi e Capuletti* as to write a criticism in the *Elegante Zeitung* scoffing at Weber's *Euryanthe*, which had just been performed in a cold and lifeless way in Leipizg.

In later life, when writing his autobiography, Wagner refers to this period, when he imitated Bellini and Auber and tolerated Meyerbeer, as a time of "æsthetic demoralisation." This attitude was natural, but it was also part of his propaganda for his own music. As the operas of Auber, Bellini and Meyerbeer are rarely performed nowadays, the musical public to-day may take Wagner at his own valuation and accept naïvely his statement that his appreciation of these works during the years from 1834 to 1838 was a sign of that "decline in my classical taste which was destined to last some considerable time." But from the artistic standpoint there is something else to be said. Bellini's *Norma* – to take one example – is an opera in which sincerity of feeling, dramatic truthfulness and musical talent are present in at least as great a degree as in Wagner's *Tannhäuser*; while such an aria as "Casta diva," in the first act of *Norma*, would be considered by most musicians to-day to be superior to "O Star of Eve" or any other aria in *Tannhäuser* – and quite as relevant dramatically. Further, if we take an

opera that, as a work of art, is, in my opinion,
far superior to *Tannhäuser*, namely, *Der Fliegende
Holländer*, we shall find in his earlier work by
Wagner the signs of his acquaintance with the
operatic style of the Italian composers such as
Bellini. It has been the fashion, following
Wagner's own attitude, to decry the second act
of *Der Fliegende Holländer* on this account, but a
less partisan, less prejudiced judgment will be
likely to find considerable and unusual charm
and merit in this second act.

The fact is that these artistic movements are
due to the natural necessity for change more than
to improvements or deterioration in taste. A
proof of this is the fact that the style of bad productions as well as of good changes from generation to generation, and every generation has its
superior and its inferior works of art. The superior
are not all in one style and the inferior in another.
To imagine that they are is to be very ignorant of
history. It is clever propagandists who try to present the public with a label by which they may
know the good from the bad. The Wagnerian
categorisation of Weber and Méhul as classical,
and Bellini and Rossini as decadent, is just non-
sense. To describe a difference in style by such
vague words as "classical" and "decadent,"
with their inappropriate association with moral
values, is to appeal to prejudice, not to reason or
perception.

In tracing the career of Wagner up to 1834,
when he was twenty-one years old, I have dealt
chiefly with the development of his musical talent,
since that is the most important part of the man.
But it is necessary to consider his nature and

character at this period, since it is not only a man's genius or talent that contributes to his artistic achievements, but all his other attributes also. According to Praeger, who knew him intimately for a great number of years and was born in the same city, Leipzig, Wagner was a delicate child and was affected with "an irritating form of erysipelas which constantly troubled him up to the time of his death." As Praeger's is, on the whole, the best and fullest description of Wagner's personal appearance, I will quote it rather fully:

"Throughout his life Wagner was always remarkably and neatly dressed, caring much for his personal appearance ... he was no sooner at school than he attracted to himself a few of the cleverest boys by his early developed gift of ready speech and sarcasm. 'Die Dummer haben mich immer gehasst' (The stupid have ever hated me) was a favourite saying of his in after life. The study of dead languages ... was a delight to him. He had a facility for languages. It was one of his gifts. History and geography also attracted him. He was an omnivorous reader, and his precise knowledge on any subject was always a matter of surprise to the most intimate. It could never be said what he had read or what he had not read; and here perhaps is the place to note a remarkable feature in Wagner's disposition, viz. his modesty. Did he require information on any subject, his manner of asking was childlike in its simplicity. He was patient in learning and mastering the point. But it should be observed that nothing short of the most complete and satisfactory explanation would satisfy him. And then would the thinking power of the man declare itself. The information he had newly acquired would be thoroughly assimilated and then given forth under a new light with a force truly remarkable."

A few words of comment on these observations are necessary. It seems misleading to ascribe Wagner's concentration on his own interests and purposes as "modesty." Would it not be nearer the mark to say that Wagner was the exact opposite of what the world calls a fool? This may be illustrated by one incident from his autobiography. Having composed his Symphony in C major at the age of nineteen, in 1832, he paid a summer holiday visit to Vienna and took his score with him. On his return home to Leipzig he stayed at Prague, made the acquaintance of the director of the Conservatorium, Dionys Weber, in order to get his symphony performed. He says:

"Truly I had to deal with a kind of 'Dionysus the Tyrant.' A man who did not acknowledge Beethoven's genius beyond his second symphony, a man who looked upon the 'Eroïca' as the acme of bad taste on the master's part, who praised Mozart alone and next to him tolerated only Lindpaintner: such a man was not easy to approach, and I had to learn the art of making use of tyrants for one's own purposes. I dissimulated: I pretended to be struck by the novelty of his ideas, never contradicted him, and, to point out the similarity of our standpoints, I referred him to the end fugue in my overture and in my symphony (both in C major), which I had only succeeded in making what they were through having studied Mozart. My reward soon followed: Dionys set to work to study my orchestral

creations with almost youthful energy. The
students of the Conservatoire were compelled to
practise with the greatest exactitude my new
symphony under his dry and terribly noisy baton.
In the presence of several of my friends, amongst
whom was also the dear old Count Pachta in his
capacity of President of the Conservatoire Committee, we actually held a first performance of the
greatest work that I had written up to that date."

A boy of nineteen who can understand men and
behave with such cool adroitness is not to be described by the word "modest." Wagner combined the simplicity of the lamb with the cunning
of the fox, but the simplicity was what we may
call the first simplicity, not the third simplicity.
That is to say it was entirely natural and un-
self-conscious. Wagner did not waste his own
energies in self-observation; he always looked at
what was in front of him, or behind him, or
around him, never at what was within him. This
primitive simplicity we shall see at work all
through his career, for he kept it – and this is an
astonishing fact, properly understood – until his
death.

Praeger gives a detailed account of his physical
appearance :

"In stature Wagner was below middle size, and
like most undersized men always held himself
strictly erect. He had an unusually wiry, muscu-
lar frame, small feet – an aristocratic feature
which did not extend to his hands. It was his
head, however, that could not fail to strike even
the least enquiring that he had to do with no
ordinary mortal. The development of the frontal
part ... impressed every one. His eyes had a

piercing power but were kindly withal and were ready to smile at a witty remark. Richard Wagner lacked eyebrows, but nature, as if to make up for this deficiency, bestowed on him a most abundant crop of bushy hair which he carefully kept brushed back. . . . His mouth was very small. He had thin lips and small teeth, signs of a determined character. The nose was large and in after life somewhat disfigured by the early acquired habit of snuff-taking. The back of his head was fully developed. . . .

"As a boy he was passionate and strong-headed. His violent temper and obstinate determination were not to be thwarted in anything he had set his mind to. Among boys such wilfulness of character was the cause of frequent dissensions. He rarely, however, came to blows, for he had a shrewd wit and was winningly entertaining in speech and with much adroitness would bend them to his whims. . . . He was known as the best tumbler and somersault-turner of the large Dresden school. Indeed he was an adept in every form of bodily exercise, and, as his animal spirits never left him, he still performed boyish tricks even when nearing threescore and ten. . . . He would frighten his mother by sliding down the banisters with daring rapidity and jumping downstairs. As he always succeeded in his feats, his mother and the other children took it for granted that he would not come to grief, and sometimes he would be asked to exhibit his unwonted skill to visitors. This no doubt increased the boy's confidence in himself – a self-reliance which never left him to the time of his death."

CHAPTER II

1834-1839

Obtains post at Magdeburg – life at a provincial theatre – meets
his future wife – begins his third opera – begins to get into
debt – gives his first concert – a complete fiasco – conducts
well-known operas – finishes *Das Liebesverbot* – first performance never takes place – Minna obtains engagement at
Königsberg – Wagner marries Minna Planer – becomes
musical-director at Riga – begins the opera *Rienzi* – loses his
position at Riga – character of Minna.

PROFITING by experience at Würzburg, Wagner,
towards the autumn of 1834, got the post of music-
director at the Magdeburg theatre where he spent
over a year. This company, which was of a fair
provincial quality, visited in the summer Rudolstadt and a watering place named Lauchstädt.
Wagner's own description of his arrival there
and his first visit to the director gives a lively
picture of a small German touring company of
the period:

"The little watering place (Lauchstädt) had
in the days of Goethe and Schiller acquired a very
wide reputation. Its wooden theatre had been
built according to the design of the former, and the
first performance of the *Braut von Messina* had been
given there. But although I repeated all this to
myself, the place made me feel rather doubtful. I
asked for the house of the director of the theatre.
He proved to be out, but a small dirty boy, his son,
was told to take me to the theatre to find 'Papa.'
Papa, however, met us on the way. He was an
elderly man; he wore a dressing-gown and on his

head a cap. His delight at greeting me was interrupted by complaints about a serious indisposi-
tion, for which his son was to fetch him a cordial
from a shop close by. Before despatching the boy
on this errand he pressed a real silver penny into
his hand with a certain ostentation which was
obviously for my benefit. This person was
Heinrich Bethmann, surviving husband of the
famous actress of that name, who, having lived in
the heyday of the German stage, had won the
favour of the King of Prussia – and won it so
lastingly that long after her death it had continued to be extended to her spouse. He always
drew a nice pension from the Prussian Court, and
permanently enjoyed its support, without being
able to forfeit its protection by his irregular and
dissipated ways."

Bethmann took Wagner to his house, where he
found Bethmann's second wife, a cripple, extended
on "an extraordinary couch, while an elderly
bass, of whose excessive devotion Bethmann had
already complained to me quite openly, smoked
his pipe beside her." Bethmann introduced
Wagner to the stage-manager, Schmale, with
whom he left him, whereupon Schmale complained that they were supposed to put on Mozart's *Don Juan* the following Sunday, but that
everything was put on his shoulders, and he did
not know how he was to get it rehearsed when the
town bandsmen of Merseberg, who formed the
orchestra, would not come over on a Saturday to
rehearse. All this had such a depressing effect on
Wagner that he made up his mind he would go
back to Leipzig. He describes how, while talking
to him, Schmale kept stretching his hand through

the open window, plucking cherries from a tree and eating them, "ejecting the stones with a disagreeable noise." Wagner adds: "It was this last circumstance in particular which decided me; for, strange to say, I have an innate aversion from fruit."

But one of those seemingly accidental encounters which alter the whole course of a person's life now took place. Wagner was taken to a lodging where the junior lead of the company, Minna Planer, was staying, and met her as it happened at the door. He describes the vivid impression made on him by her fresh and charming personality and the "startling effect" of her scrupulous neatness and tidiness. The result was that he decided to stay, and so his career as a conductor began with the Magdeburg company. Wagner had never yet conducted an opera, his experience of conducting was confined to one or two performances of his own works, yet he managed to scrape through passably enough; although, when the company went to Rudolstadt, the leader of the royal orchestra conducted, and Wagner was occupied in rehearsing the operas and musical plays required in the repertory. He began at the same time to write the libretto of his third opera, *Das Liebesverbot*. On the return of the company for the winter season at Magdeburg, he got his first real experience as a conductor, and some concerts were given under his direction in 1835, at which his overture to *Die Feen*, a new overture, *Columbus*, and other minor compositions were performed.

In the meantime an intimate friendship had developed between him and the young actress

Minna Planer, whose modesty and decency marked her out from the majority of the company. His own comments, nearly forty years later in *Mein Leben*, on his early relations with Minna Planer, who later on became his first wife, are not always to be taken as literally true. They were written under the eye of his second wife, Cosima, and Wagner wrote *Mein Leben* in self-justification. Like everything he put on paper throughout his life, it is a piece of special pleading in which he is always dexterously placed in the best possible or the most effective light. He describes in *Mein Leben* a convivial party, which he gave at Magdeburg, to which he invited Minna:

"I had already warned my landlord that we were not likely to be very quiet and reassured him as to any possible damage to his furniture. What the champagne failed to accomplish the punch eventually succeeded in doing; all the restraints of petty conventionality, which the company usually endeavoured to observe, were cast aside ... and then it was that Minna's great dignity distinguished her from all her companions. She never lost her self-respect; and, whilst no one ventured to take the slightest liberty with her, every one very clearly recognised the simple candour with which she responded to my kindly and solicitous attentions. They could not fail to see that the link existing between us was not to be compared to any ordinary *liaison*, and we had the satisfaction of seeing the flighty young lady who had openly angled for me fall into a fit over the discovery."

Wagner gives an amusing description of the development of his relationship with Minna

Planer. He used to meet her in company with a
clever but elderly actress, Mme Haas, and on one
occasion he had promised Minna to spend the
evening with her and Mme Haas; but by this
time Mme Haas had become disagreeable to him
on account of her jealousy and criticism of Minna,
so, having gone to a whist party first, he stayed as
long as possible in the hope that Mme Haas would
have departed. He says:

"The only way I could do this was by drinking
hard, so that I had the very unusual experience of
rising from a sober party in a completely fuddled
condition, into which I had imperceptibly fallen
and in which I refused to believe. This incre-
dulity deluded me into keeping my engagement.
. . . To my intense disgust the elder woman
was still there . . . and her presence at once had
the effect of rousing my tipsiness to a violent outbreak; for she seemed astonished at my rowdy
and unseemly behaviour and made several remarks upon it intended for jokes, whereupon I
scoffed at her in the coarsest manner, so that
she immediately left the house in high dudgeon.
I had still sense enough to be conscious of Minna's
astonished laughter at my outrageous conduct."

As Wagner was in no fit state to be removed,
Minna looked after him and resigned her own
bed to him. When he awoke in the morning he
says:

"On recognising where I was, I at once realised
and grew more convinced of the fact that this
morning's sunrise marked the starting point of an
infinitely momentous period of my life. The
demon of care had at last entered into my
existence.

"Without any light-hearted jests, without gaiety or joking of any description we breakfasted quietly and decorously together, and at an hour when, in view of the compromising circumstances of the previous evening, we could set out without attracting undue notice, I set off with Minna for a long walk beyond the city gates. Then we parted, and from that day forward freely and openly gratified our desires as an acknowledged pair of lovers."

At Magdeburg at the early age of twenty-two Wagner had his first experience of acquiring debts on a liberal scale, of optimistically arranging grandiose and expensive means of settling them, and of finding his optimism totally unjustified, resulting in his being left in a worse position than ever. As this was to be his habitual method of procedure throughout his life until, when over fifty years old, he found the almost bottomless purse of a king behind him, it is necessary to give a full account of his initiation in the art of living by means of music of the future, on money of the future. He had induced the famous singer Mme Schröder-Devrient to come from Leipzig to give a few special performances, and she appeared as Desdemona and Romeo with Wagner conducting. He found her inspiring as usual and so sympathetic – as such a fine artist would naturally be to a young man of talent – that she actually offered to sing at a benefit concert for him. The only person in the Magdeburg theatre company who drew his full salary was the bass whom Wagner had found smoking by the couch of the director's wife, and, as Wagner was already heavily in debt, he began feverishly to prepare for settling his affairs by means of a splendid concert.

He told his creditors of the fabulous receipts he expected and invited them to come and be paid at the hotel, to which he had moved at the close of the season, the day after the concert.

As he says, it was not unreasonable of him to expect a full house, but – and this is what is so characteristic of Wagner, especially when we consider his age at the time – instead of keeping his expenses low in order to make as much money as possible, he was determined to have everything done in the most splendid manner. He engaged a much larger orchestra, arranged many rehearsals and made the most grandiose preparations; but the public did not believe that such a famous operatic star as Schröder-Devrient was really coming just to please the unknown little Magdeburg conductor; also they objected to the high prices charged. The result was a very poor audience. Schröder-Devrient sang Beethoven's "Adelaïde" wherein, says Wagner, "to my own astonishment I accompanied her on the piano," and the programme included Wagner's own *Columbus* overture and Beethoven's "Schlacht bei Vittoria." The *Columbus* overture, with six trumpets, had already startled such audience as there was, but Beethoven's battle-piece – in which Wagner had thoroughly let himself go, doubling and trebling the trumpets and bugles and having obtained special and costly apparatus for the musketry and cannon firing – put the audience, including Mme Schröder-Devrient, to flight. "Everyone rushed out," says Wagner, "and Wellington's victory was finally celebrated in a confidential outburst between myself and the orchestra alone."

After this fiasco Wagner sought comfort, he

says, in the arms of his sorrowing sweetheart and nerved himself for the battle with his creditors, who, on the next day, gathered in rows along the corridors of his hotel. All the proceeds of the concert, together with something extra out of Wagner's pocket, went to paying the orchestra, so he invited a competent Jewess, a Mme Gottschalk, to deal with his creditors on the strength of his supposedly well-to-do connections in Leipzig. By this means he got a little temporary peace and, the season being ended, he returned to his home in Leipzig, leaving Minna to visit her parents in Dresden.

In September they returned to their Magdeburg engagement, where, that winter, Wagner had the happy experience of preparing and conducting a number of operas, including Spohr's *Jessonde*, Bellini's *Norma*, and Auber's *Lestocq*. Wagner's ingenuity and energy in obtaining good performances with the aid of the best Prussian regimental band and military singers kept the Magdeburg season afloat, in spite of the irregularities of the director Bethmann. As an example of what he achieved he says that, years later, "I was able to assure Auber, whom I often met over an ice in Tortini's café in Paris, that in his *Lestocq* I had been able to render the part of the mutinous soldiery, when seduced into conspiracy, with an absolutely full number of voices, a fact for which he thanked me with astonishment and delight."

In the meantime, by the beginning of 1836, he had completed his opera, *Liebesverbot*, the libretto of which is founded on Shakespeare's *Measure for Measure*. Things were going from bad to worse in the theatre on account of the director's chronic

C

insolvency. In March, owing to non-payment of salaries, the most popular members of the company resigned, having found employment elsewhere. As a personal favour to Wagner they consented to stay till the end of March to perform his new opera. The work was prepared in ten days. About a quarter of an hour before the performance began Wagner anxiously surveyed the auditorium and discovered only Mme Gottschalk, her husband, and a Polish Jew in full evening dress seated in the stalls. Hopeful as ever, Wagner reckoned there was still a quarter of an hour in which the house might fill, when suddenly a terrible uproar broke out behind the scenes. The husband of the prima donna – having surveyed the house from behind the curtain with Wagner and satisfied himself that it was practically empty and that he would not be harming his colleague – decided that his hour of revenge had come and had suddenly assaulted the second tenor, who was his wife's lover. The second tenor was put out of action for the evening, and the wife went into convulsions. The manager had to go before the curtain and explain to the scanty audience that, "owing to unforeseen circumstances," the performance could not take place.

This was the climax of Wagner's career at Magdeburg. Every time he returned home he found a summons nailed to his door, but Minna was, as always, helpful and practical. She obtained an engagement at the Königsberg theatre, and, although the post of musical conductor was filled, the directors, in order to obtain her services, promised Wagner an approaching vacancy. Eventually Wagner obtained

the definite promise of the conductorship, and on
the strength of this he married Minna Planer on
November 24th, 1836. After about a year at
Königsberg the director of the theatre became
insolvent, and Wagner and his wife were left
stranded once more; but he luckily obtained a
position as conductor at a theatre at Riga, which
was a much more prosperous place than either
Magdeburg or Königsberg. Here he stayed for
the full time of his contract, namely, two years,
and produced many operas including Méhul's
Joseph, a work which inspired him with fresh
enthusiasm. It was during these two years at
Riga that Wagner returned to his earlier and
more idealistic vein. He wrote the book and
composed the first two acts of his fourth opera,
Rienzi, and began to lead less of the Bohemian
life of the average member of a theatrical company. As a consequence he fell foul of the directors
of the theatre, whose taste was for light and
frivolous entertainments, and this was the reason
that in 1839 his contract was not renewed.

In this development of Wagner's character the
part played by his wife, Minna, must not be overlooked. There will be occasion to discuss later,
more fully, the character of Minna, but at this
stage it is necessary to relate several incidents of
their life together between the date of his marriage
in 1836 and the year of his leaving Riga, 1839.
We have to rely chiefly on Wagner's own account
in *Mein Leben* of the early years of his marriage,
and this account cannot – in view of Wagner's
own unreliability – be taken as completely accurate. It is, however, unlikely to be false in fact so
much as in interpretation and tone. As Minna

was – considering all things – the most important woman in his life, it is necessary to try to obtain a clear picture of her.

Praeger, who knew her and was a warm friend of her husband, had no reason to give anything but his honest opinion of her, and this is what he says in *Wagner as I knew Him*:

"Minna was handsome but not strikingly so. Of medium height, slim figure, she had a pair of soft gazelle-like eyes which were a faithful index of a tender heart. Her look seemed to bespeak your clemency, and her gentle speech secured at once your good will. Her movements in the house were devoid of anything approaching bustle. Quick to anticipate your thoughts, your wish was complied with before it had been expressed. Her bearing was that of the gentle nurse in the sick chamber. It was joy to be tended by her. She was full of heart's affection, and Wagner let himself be loved. Her nature was the opposite of his. He was passionate, strong-willed and ambitious: she was gentle, docile and contented. . . . To his exuberant speech, his constant discourses on art and his position in the future, she lent a willing attentive ear. She could not follow him, she was unable to reason his incipient revolutionary art notions, to combat his seemingly extravagant theories; but to all she was sympathetic, sanguine and consoling – 'a perfect woman, nobly planned,' as Wordsworth sweetly sings.

"As years rolled by, and the genius of Wagner assumed more definite shape and grew in strength, she was less able to comprehend. . . . We were sitting at lunch in the trimly kept Swiss chalet at Zurich, in the summer of 1856, waiting for the composer of the completed *Rienzi, Dutchman, Tann-häuser* and *Lohengrin* to come down from his scoring of the 'Nibelungen,' when in full innocence she asked me, 'Now, honestly, is Richard such a great genius?' On another occasion, when he was bitterly animadverting on his treatment by the public, she said, 'Well, Richard, why don't you write something for the gallery?'... She had one quality of surpassing value in any household presided over by a man of Wagner's thoughtless extravagance. She was thrifty and economical...."

A fact known to few people but Wagner for many years was that at the age of seventeen Minna had an illegitimate daughter. This daughter, named Nathalie, always passed as her sister, and, as late as 1862, according to Wagner, she was still ignorant that Minna was her mother. In order to maintain herself and her daughter, Minna, who had attracted attention probably more by her appearance than by her acting at some private theatricals, got an engagement at the Dessau Court Theatre. Wagner says, "She had not the slightest passion for the stage, and merely saw in a theatrical career the means of earning a quick and possibly a rich livelihood."

Her attitude was the intensely practical one of a woman who has nobody to depend upon but herself and is compelled to earn her own and her daughter's living. Wagner was deeply attached to her and suffered a good deal from this attitude. His own account of her behaviour is given at some length in *Mein Leben* and demands quotation:

"The friendship of the director, manager, and favourite members of the theatre she regarded as indispensable, whilst those frequenters of the theatre who through their criticism or taste influence the public, and thus also had weight with the management, she recognised as beings upon whom the attainment of her most fervent desires depended. Never to make enemies of them appeared so natural and so necessary that, in order to maintain her popularity, she was prepared to sacrifice even her self-respect. She had in this way created for herself a certain peculiar code of behaviour that, on the one hand prompted her to avoid scandals, but on the other found excuses for making herself conspicuous, as long as she herself knew that she was doing nothing wrong. Hence arose a mixture of inconsistence the questionable sense of which she was incapable of grasping. It was clearly impossible for her not to lose all real sense of delicacy; she showed, however, a sense of fitness of things which made her have regard to what was considered proper, though she could not understand that mere appearances were a mockery when they only served to cloak the absence of a real sense of delicacy. As she was without idealism, she had no artistic feeling; neither did she possess any talent for acting, and her power of pleasing was due entirely to her charming appearance."

Appropriate comment on this plausible analysis of Minna's behaviour is that it is the work of a born actor, which Minna was not. More delicacy is undoubtedly expected from women than from men. Wagner showed in the course of his life that delicacy was not one of his qualities; his lack of sensitiveness was at least as great as Minna's, but, whereas Minna did not pretend to do anything more than adapt herself to circumstances with as little loss of her self-respect as possible,

Wagner always succeeded in explaining away his indelicate behaviour as the fault of other people. His criticism of Minna shows him at his worst, because we see revealed in it the nature of his dramatic talent: a talent not of that high order which demands a profound truthfulness and understanding of life, but of that lesser kind which is fertile in the invention of plausible and effective attitudes based, not on the reality of true feeling, but on moral and philosophical fiction, or what Wagner called "idealism."

It is interesting to find that Wagner is so little aware of the real character of his behaviour that he actually gives himself away completely in the few sentences which follow the above analysis, when he says:

"The strange power she exercised over me from the very first was in no wise due to the fact that I regarded her in any way as the embodiment of my ideal; on the contrary, she attracted me by the soberness and seriousness of her character, which supplemented what I felt to be wanting in my own, and afforded me the support that in my wanderings after the ideal I knew to be necessary for me."

It is in this latter paragraph that we get an indication of Wagner's charm, which must have been very real and strong, judging by the numbers of people who succumbed to it throughout his life. He was extraordinarily natural and in a primitive sense simple. In mere greed for what he wanted he did not stop to think, all his thinking was directed towards getting what he wanted. If Minna was sober and serious, he was himself flamboyant and frivolous, and in spite of his

genius there was reason in Minna's apt query to
Praeger: "Now, honestly, is Richard such a
great genius?" In Minna's lifetime the answer
was "yes"; but we are already beginning to see
the point of Minna's enquiry, and I believe that
the answer of posterity – if Minna were able to put
her question again – would be "no." For if
Wagner had genius – and, no doubt, we must
apply the word to him – he was, nevertheless,
both as a musician and an artist, less great than
the Wagnerians thought.

Since Wagner made public to the world, in his
autobiography published after his death, facts
which might never have been known otherwise –
such for example as the secret so carefully preserved by Minna of her illegitimate child and the
occasion of Minna's unfaithfulness to him after
their marriage, when she left him at Königsberg
in despair – it is necessary to represent Minna's
point of view as far as it is known. Her own explanation of the latter incident, in a letter quoted
by Dr. Julius Knapp in his *The Women in Wagner's
Life*, is as follows:

"True, my love for Richard had gone from me
during that critical time; yet I do not believe
that things would have gone so far had not a certain man in good circumstances come along just
then, who displayed such a strong appearance of
heartfelt and anxious sympathy for me in my
painful position and assured me of that sympathy
in such a seductive manner that, for the time
being, I wavered under all these conflicting impressions. I could no longer see in Richard's love
for me – particularly now that it found expression
only in such painful excesses as to be hardly

recognisable – an adequate compensation for all the misery which this unhappy, inopportune marriage had brought on us both."

This was the only occasion in her life (it took place within a year after their marriage) when Minna failed Wagner. Their financial situation was desperate, his conduct violent and reckless, and the future seemed hopeless. But she soon found out her mistake, and, as the bond between them was stronger than any other, she returned to him in Riga, in October 1837, with her reputed sister Nathalie. From that time on her attitude to him is best expressed in her own letter to their friend Apel about a year later, when their position in Paris was desperate:

"Even had I the means to leave Paris, I would not dream of leaving Richard in his present position, for I know that it was not recklessness that brought him to it, but the noble and natural ambition of an artist, and that any artist is likely to suffer the same fate without some special help. I only consented to his plan of going to Paris after great protest; but the more I see of his projects here, the more am I convinced that if he goes under, if he fails in the aim he might otherwise attain, it will be solely for lack of sufficient support. . . . You may be sure I do not usually share Richard's exalted hopes, but this time I know from his own lips that he is only a step removed from the achievement of his aim. . . . There is in Richard great talent to be saved, which is in danger of being wasted, for he has already reached the point of losing his courage completely – without that his higher destiny will be missed. It may well be that a heavy responsibility rests on those who now turn away from him with a shrug. I cannot give him up, and I am, therefore, perhaps, the only person who vividly feels how disgraceful it is to let him come to grief."

Such was the woman "without idealism," who had "no artistic feelings." Her conduct was as good as her word, not only during their privations in Paris but also many years later. It is also necessary, in justice to Wagner, to remark that in spite of behaviour towards Minna which was often inconsiderate and selfish, he was extremely fond of her, and his affectionate and cheerful society must have partly compensated her for many troubles.

CHAPTER III

1839–1842

Escapes from his creditors – crossing the Russian frontier – sails for London – storms drive ship to refuge in Norway – origin of *The Flying Dutchman* – arrives in London – visits the Houses of Parliament – asks for Bulwer Lytton – hears the Duke of Wellington speak – opinions of London and the English – sails for Boulogne – visits Meyerbeer – arrives in Paris – hears Beethoven's Ninth Symphony – reduced to great poverty – completes *Rienzi* and sketches libretto of *The Flying Dutchman* – meets Berlioz – starts on music to *The Flying Dutchman* – does hack work to earn a living – hears that *Rienzi* is accepted by the Dresden Opera House – meets Heine – Wagner and Berlioz.

In July 1839 Wagner left Riga, with the object of going to Paris with his partially completed opera *Rienzi* and trying his luck there. As he was heavily in debt it was not easy for him to leave without settling with his creditors in Königsberg and Magdeburg as well as in Riga. He raised a little money by selling his household furniture, but this, together with the sum received from a benefit concert and some meagre savings, would only have sufficed, he says, to satisfy his creditors. An old friend named Möller gave him the welcome advice to keep this money for his Paris adventure and pay his creditors with the proceeds of his Paris successes. But to get away without paying his creditors was not so easy. With the aid of Möller he made a plan to cross the Russian frontier secretly by carriage and get to the East Prussian port of Pillau. Their foreign passports had been seized by their creditors, so elaborate arrangements had to be made to get safely across.

They were further encumbered by a large New-foundland dog, which had become devoted to Wagner in Riga and for which room in the carriage had to be found. After two days' travelling through Courland, they reached the Russo-Prussian frontier towards evening. Wagner, Minna and the dog were then led on foot through by-paths to a smugglers' drinking den which, says Wagner, "gradually became filled to suffocation with Polish Jews of most forbidding aspect."

After sundown a guide took them to the slope of a hill where there was a ditch running the whole length of the frontier and guarded by Cossacks. During the relief of the watch they had to run down the hill, scramble through the ditch and then get out of range of the guns of the soldiers, who were commanded to fire on fugitives at sight. All this they achieved safely but not without great anxiety and exhaustion, and Wagner charac-teristically remarks: "I was simply at a loss to convey to my poor exhausted wife how extremely I regretted the whole affair." The carriage they had arranged for turned up and took them to a Prussian village, where they met their friend Möller, "positively sick with anxiety." The next day they crossed the plain of Tilsit to Arnau, where they rested a few days. As there were no railways and it was impossible to take the dog by coach to Paris, and also too expensive for them-selves, they arranged to go by sailing vessel from Pillau to London. To avoid Königsberg they had to leave the main roads, with the consequence that the carriage upset, and Minna, says Wagner,

"was so severely indisposed by the accident . . .
that I had to drag her – with the greatest difficulty
as she was quite helpless – to a peasant's house.
The people were surly and dirty, and the night
was a painful one for the poor sufferer." They
arranged to go in an English sailing vessel, the
Thetis, and after a few days' rest, during which
Minna recovered, they had to evade the harbour
watch and the officials visiting the ship and slip
on board unseen, by means of a small boat, before
daybreak. The *Thetis* carried a crew of seven
men, including the captain, and in good summer
weather would make London in about eight days;
but, with Wagner on board, nothing so un-
dramatic was going to happen, and the voyage
actually took three weeks and a half, during which
they encountered two storms, ran against a reef
and had twice to take refuge in a Norwegian fjord.

Wagner's own account of this trip is extremely
vivid and amusing. When they first took refuge
on the Norwegian coast, he says, "a feeling of
indescribable content came over me when the
enormous granite walls echoed the hail of the
crew as they cast anchor and furled the sails. The
sharp rhythm of this call clung to me like an omen
of good cheer and shaped itself presently into the
theme of the seamen's song in my *Fliegende Holländer*. The idea of this opera was, even at that
time, ever present in my mind, and it now took
on a definite poetic and musical colour. . . ."

Three weeks and a half, tossing through storms
on the North Sea in a small sailing ship, is no
joke, but Wagner describes how he was in the best
of spirits as soon as they anchored in the mouth of
the Thames and shaved himself on deck near the

mast, while Minna and the exhausted crew slept.
They took a steamer from Gravesend to London
Bridge, where they landed and went to the Horse-
shoe Tavern, near the Tower. They left this for
the King's Arms in Old Compton Street and
spent a week seeing the sights of the city, which
delighted them by its size and liveliness. Wagner
immediately tried to find Sir George Smart (whom
he calls Sir John Smart in *Mein Leben*), of the
Royal Philharmonic Society, to whom he had
sent his "Rule Britannia" overture. "It is
true," says Wagner, "that he had never acknowledged it, but I felt it the more incumbent on me
to bring him to task about it." Sir George, however, was not in London, so Wagner then decided
to look up Bulwer Lytton, the author of the novel
Rienzi which he had dramatised. He had heard
abroad that Bulwer Lytton was a member of
Parliament, so he went to the House of Commons.
Fortunately, as he says, he could not speak one
word of English, and, since none of the minor
officials could make out what he wanted, he was
passed on to higher and higher authorities, until
some "distinguished-looking man" spoke to him
in French and seemed "favourably impressed"
when Wagner asked for Bulwer Lytton. The
famous author was not, however, in London, but
Wagner, by pressing, got admission to the
strangers' gallery in the House of Lords.

"I was immensely interested to see the Premier,
Lord Melbourne, and Brougham (who seemed to
me to take a very active part in the proceedings,
prompting Melbourne several times as I thought)
and the Duke of Wellington, who looked so comfortable in his grey beaver hat, with his hands

diving deep into his trousers pockets, and who made his speech in so conversational a tone that I lost my feeling of excessive awe. . . . The matter in hand was, as I learned afterwards from the papers, the discussion of measures to be taken against the Portuguese Government to ensure the passing of the Anti-Slavery Bill. The Bishop of London . . . was the only one of these gentlemen whose voice and manner seemed to me stiff or unnatural, but possibly I was prejudiced by my dislike of parsons generally."

Wagner did not go to the Italian opera because of the high prices, but thoroughly explored the city, "shuddered through a ghastly London Sunday, and wound up with a train trip (our very first) to Gravesend Park in the company of the captain of the *Thetis*."

His opinions of London and the English, based on his first visit in 1839 and his second visit (to conduct the Philharmonic Society concerts) in 1855, as related by Praeger, who was living in London in 1855 and saw him then constantly, are not without interest. He disliked the size of London and had definite opinions as to the proper limits of a city, saying that none should be larger than Dresden; he thought the English strangely contradictory in their character, habits and institutions; but in later life he expressed the opinion that they were "the most poetic of European nations." Whereas the Germans sought after a cultivated poetry and it lay more on the surface in France, it was deep in the hearts of the English. It is interesting to learn that what chiefly convinced Wagner of the correctness of this idea was the employment of the disabled battleship

Dreadnought, from Nelson's fleet at Trafalgar, as
a home for worn-out seamen – which he described
as "incontestable proof of a poetic sentiment."
The quiet unobtrusive manner of the English
pleased Minna but irritated Wagner, who complained of their stolidity, stiffness and inexpres-
siveness. On August 20th, 1839, they crossed by
steamer to Boulogne. As it was too early for
important people to be back in Paris, and the
composer Meyerbeer was in Boulogne, they took
two unfurnished rooms at a wine merchant's,
half an hour from Boulogne on the Paris road,
and fixed themselves with a bed, two chairs and
a table on which Wagner worked at the instrumentation of *Rienzi*, after they had eaten the meals
they prepared themselves.

Wagner next called on Meyerbeer and found
him friendly. He liked his appearance – "the
years had not yet given his features the flabby
look which sooner or later mars most Jewish faces,
and the fine formation of his brow round about
the eyes gave him an expression of countenance
that inspired confidence." Meyerbeer let Wagner
read him the libretto of *Rienzi* and then heard the
two acts of the music, which Wagner played in
his own peculiar style, as already described. There
is no doubt that the dramatic talent of Wagner
impressed Meyerbeer considerably, since it was
along his own lines of vivid pageantry and melo-
drama, and he gave him letters of introduction
with which he set out for Paris. As usual, however, even this brief and friendly intercourse was
not without an occasion for Wagner's spleen.
Meyerbeer praised his minute and neat hand-
writing of the score. Those who have seen any

of the originals, or the reproduced facsimiles, of
Wagner's scores will not be surprised that they
should have often been praised, for their clarity
and spotless neatness is really remarkable, in great
contrast to the scores of Beethoven, or even
Mozart's. But to praise the appearance of his
scores to Wagner was not unnaturally an unpardonable offence.

The first impression Wagner got from Paris was
disappointing. It seemed narrow and mean after
London. The Rue de la Tonnellerie, which
linked the Rue St. Honoré with the Marché des
Innocents, where a furnished room had been
engaged for him, was so small and dingy that he
says he felt "positively degraded" at having to
live there; but he cheered up when he saw a bust
of Molière on the front of the house, with an inscription "maison où naquit Molière." He took
his letter of introduction to Duponchel, the
director of the Opera, but Duponchel, "fixing
a monocle in his right eye . . . read through
Meyerbeer's letter without displaying the least
emotion," and Wagner never heard from him
again. He called on Habeneck, the famous conductor, who was more friendly and promised to
perform his *Columbus* overture at one of the
orchestral practices at the Conservatoire. This
he actually did, but, Wagner says, "there was
no question of producing this work, even at one
of the celebrated Conservatoire concerts; I saw
clearly that the old gentleman was only moved
by kindness and a desire to encourage me. It
could not lead to anything further, and I myself was convinced that this extremely superficial work of my young days could only

D

give the orchestra a wrong impression of my talents."

During his attendance at these rehearsals he heard this famous orchestra and conductor preparing a performance of Beethoven's Ninth Symphony, and their playing of this great work made a tremendous impression on him, which he says he could only compare with the revelation made to him when as a youth of sixteen he heard Schröder-Devrient in *Fidelio*. It stirred in him a fresh longing to compose, and the immediate result was a sketch for his well-known *Faust* overture, which he rewrote fifteen years later on the advice of Liszt, who gave him "many valuable hints." On Meyerbeer's arrival in Paris, Wagner visited him and, through him, made several acquaintances, such as the publisher, Maurice Schlesinger; but Meyerbeer returned to Germany, and, after six months in Paris, Wagner had exhausted all his money, although they lived very economically, "dining at a very small restaurant at a franc a head." Minna, says Praeger, "cleaned the house, stood at the wash-tub, did the mending and cooking," and was always cheerful and uncomplaining. They were forced to pawn everything they possessed and then to sell the pawn-tickets. For Wagner's birthday, on May 22nd, 1840, Minna, having searched everywhere, found a small German tailor who provided her with a new suit of clothes for Wagner and agreed to wait for payment till better times. Through his friend Laub, who had married a rich widow and came to Paris in 1840, some friends and relations in Leipzig were persuaded to provide Wagner with funds for six months so that Wagner took a flat in the Rue du Helder, where Minna managed the household much more economically, having always complained of the foolishness and extravagance of living in furnished rooms and eating in restaurants. In the meantime Wagner continued the composition of *Rienzi* and began sketching the plan of the libretto of *The Flying Dutchman*.

Gradually they came to the end of their resources without Wagner having made any opening for himself in Paris. One morning, when he and Minna had been consulting how to raise the money for the quarter's rent, a parcel unexpectedly arrived by carrier. It seemed a marvellous act of Providence, and Wagner impatiently broke the seal just as a receipt-book was thrust before him with a demand for seven francs. He had seen enough to recognise that it contained his manuscript overture "Rule Britannia," returned from the London Philharmonic Society, and in a fury he refused to take it in and never saw it again. Wagner earned a certain amount of money by writing for Schlesinger's *Gazette Musicale* and doing pianoforte arrangements of operatic scores by Halévy. He also was compelled to dispose of his sketches for the book of *The Flying Dutchman* for the sum of £20 to the director of the Opera, Pillet, who wanted it for another composer. He managed to earn more money by arranging for the pianoforte Donizetti's opera *La Favorita*, which had just made a great hit in Paris. In this way, and with the assistance of Minna's excellent management, he was enabled to complete the score of *Rienzi* and send it to the Dresden Opera House. On February 4th, 1841,

at a concert given under the auspices of the
Gazette Musicale, his *Columbus* overture was performed. It was a complete failure. Berlioz, with
whom Wagner had become acquainted, was present at the rehearsal, and when it was over his
only comment was, Wagner tells us, "that it was
very difficult to get on in Paris." Their position
gradually got worse and worse, and Minna not
only had to do all the work of the household (they
had taken a lodger to diminish their expenses),
but even to clean the lodger's boots. Presently
a piece of luck came their way: they were able
to let their apartment for a few months and went
to Meudon, an inexpensive place outside Paris.
Here, in the summer of 1841, Wagner made a
start with the composition of the music to *The
Flying Dutchman*. He was able to hire a pianoforte, which he had been without for months, and
in seven weeks the whole of the music except
orchestration was completed. Lehrs, a classical
scholar, who was, like Wagner himself, miserably
poor, was a close friend all through Wagner's
sojourn in Paris. He was delighted with the
libretto and declared that *Der Fliegende Holländer*
would be Wagner's *Don Juan*. This is of interest,
as it forecasts present opinion. Lehrs seems to
have been one of those modest, highly intelligent
men who make no name in the world and whose
abilities are often exploited by their inferiors in
talent but superiors in insensitiveness and greed.
To-day there are critics who think as Lehrs
thought, and I myself, after a long experience of
Wagner's operas, have come at last to find in *The
Flying Dutchman* a freshness, directness, spontaneity
and sincerity that I do not find in Wagner's later

works. It may not be fanciful to imagine that these qualities are present partly because Wagner, confined in stuffy narrow quarters and with his early optimistic hopes of Paris shattered, was in a more genuinely idealistic, creative mood. Also that the couple of years which had elapsed since his first and only vivid experience of the sea was just the right amount of time for that assimilation of experience which is necessary before there can be fruitful artistic creation.

When the Wagners returned to Paris on October 30th, 1841, their financial plight was if possible more desperate than ever. He had finished most of the instrumentation of *The Flying Dutchman* but still had the overture to compose, and he managed this with the help of his friend Kietz, who was able to get money enough, in "instalments of five or ten francs," to keep them going until December, when the score of *The Flying Dutchman* was completed and sent to the Berlin Court Theatre. Wagner then had to find journalistic work to provide the bare necessities of existence, and he struggled on in a hand to mouth way until February 1842, when he received definite news that the Dresden Opera House had accepted and were going to perform *Rienzi*. Wagner, with the practical energy which never failed him, determined that his presence in Dresden was advisable, to make certain of the production of his opera as well as to supervise it. He succeeded in borrowing the money to go to Dresden from his brother-in-law, Friedrich Brockhaus, and, on April 7th, 1842, he and Minna left Paris, after a stay of two years and five months.

Wagner was now twenty-nine years old, and his

stay in Paris was probably the most formative period of his life, artistically. In the first place he heard the best orchestral and operatic music that Paris could offer, and Paris was the principal musical centre of the world at that time. In spite of his statement that he did not often visit the Opera, he admits that he was "dazzled" by the production of Meyerbeer's *Huguenots* and much impressed by its "beautiful orchestral execution and the extremely careful and effective *mise en scène*." He probably did not gain much from personal association with the intelligent world of Paris, although he became acquainted with such remarkable men as the poet Heine and the composers Halévy and Berlioz. It was from Berlioz that Wagner gained most. Berlioz is the only one of Wagner's musical contemporaries of whose compositions he speaks in *Mein Leben* with any real respect. It is difficult to know how much a creative artist ever learns technically from his contemporaries. I am inclined to think that it is very little positively, but it may be more negatively. That is to say he may learn what to avoid, what are the banalities and platitudes of his age; and he may learn this, not from those who commit them, but from one or two superior artists of his generation whose work is free from them and has rarer qualities.

As Berlioz was one of the most extraordinary men of the nineteenth century and the greatest musical genius France has so far produced, his relations with Wagner are of considerable interest. According to Praeger they were not altogether happy in each other's society, and it is worth quoting Praeger's own words, remembering that he refers to a later period when they were both in London at the same time:

"From close observation of the two men under my roof, at the same table . . . I should say that the constraint arose purely from their antagonistic individualities. Berlioz was reserved, self-possessed and dignified. His clear transparent delivery was as the rhythmic cadence of a fountain. Wagner was boisterous, effusive, and his words leaped forth as the rushing of a mountain torrent . . . the two men met often but were mutually antagonistic. They admired each other always. Both were serious and earnest but their friendship was never intimate. In after life the same strained bearing towards each other was maintained."

Wagner first heard Berlioz's music in Paris, in the winter of 1839–40, when Berlioz conducted three performances of his new symphony "Romeo and Juliet." Later on he heard the "Symphonie Fantastique," "Harold en Italie" and the "Symphonie Funèbre et Triomphale." It is quite clear from the tone of Wagner's remarks in *Mein Leben*, written more than a quarter of a century later, that he was absolutely overwhelmed by the power and originality of these works. He even goes so far as to say, "It is a fact that at the time I felt almost like a little schoolboy by the side of Berlioz. . . . I was simply all ears for things of which till then I had never dreamt, and which I felt I must try to realise."

It is not surprising that Wagner should use these terms. Most able musicians to-day find Berlioz's music just as original and astonishing as Wagner did. In the hundred years which have passed since Berlioz wrote the "Symphonie Fantastique" there has not been any diminution of interest in his music among professional musicians, rather the contrary; whilst there is something of an ebb in the appeal of Wagner's music. In spite, however, of the fact that Wagner heard some of Berlioz's finest compositions when he was under thirty years old and was still eager to learn, there is surprisingly little sign in his later works of Berlioz's influence. His own character and style are so totally different that what he learned from Berlioz was rather of a general nature. Berlioz undoubtedly made him realise for the first time the possibilities of prodigious new effects with the modern orchestra, and, once having had a glimpse of these possibilities, he developed his orchestration along his own lines leading to those wonderful effects of colour, sonority and descriptive writing which play the chief rôle in the "Ring," *Tristan und Isolde* and *Parsifal*. Nevertheless, Wagner's orchestration is much more on the lines of Weber than of Berlioz. The style of Berlioz is more austere: he is content with a hint and a delicate imaginative touch where Wagner pours forth his whole vocabulary and empties his palette. It is hardly surprising that the passionate and sceptical mind of Berlioz should not have harmonised very well with the histrionic and naïve intelligence of Wagner. Wagner never lost his zest for life and for the ordinary pleasures of life. It is one of his most unusual and attractive characteristics. But one feels that Berlioz was very early a disillusioned man. He did not believe in himself in the simple way Wagner believed in himself and, not believing in himself, it was hardly surprising that he did not believe in Wagner – a fact of which Wagner would quickly have become conscious – and this alone was cause enough for uneasiness between them.

In order to make clear the sort of confidence I am speaking of, I ought perhaps to put it in another way. It was necessary for Wagner's belief in himself that he should see it justified in the eyes of the world – hence his unresting energy in obtaining recognition and performances of his work on a grand scale. Berlioz's belief in his work was both more self-sufficient and more modest. Berlioz could not have failed to be aware that his work was not ordinary, but he shows more love of music than himself in his work; whereas it is true, is it not, that Wagner's work shows just the contrary preoccupation.

It has been customary to see the two men Berlioz and Wagner in quite a different light. Praeger says that Berlioz was jealous of Wagner, and he quotes August Röckel's description of the meeting between Berlioz and Wagner, when the former came to Dresden, in 1842, to hear *Rienzi* and *The Flying Dutchman*. "Satisfied he was not"; says Praeger, "about the only number he thought meritorious was the prayer. With the 'Dutchman' . . . he was still less contented. He complained of the excess of instrumentation." Praeger thinks this is very curious in a composer who employs "four orchestras with twelve kettledrums in one work," but surely this is a wilful blindness, for Berlioz's instrumentation always fits the purpose and is oftener light and spare than heavy; whereas Wagner's tends to excessive elaboration. Röckel, who was second music-director **at** Dresden under Wagner and worshipped his chief, thinking him much the greatest living composer, described the behaviour of Berlioz and Wagner together in detail in letters to Praeger, who gives their content as follows:

"Wagner was at first attracted, but the cold, austere, though always polished demeanour of Berlioz checked Wagner's enthusiasm. He had the air of patronising Wagner; his speech was bitter, freezing the boisterous expansiveness of Wagner. At times the conversation was so strained that Röckel was of opinion that Berlioz intentionally slighted Wagner. The more they were together, the less they appeared to understand each other, and yet, notwithstanding the fastidious criticism, the constant fault-finding, of Berlioz, he took pains to arrange meetings with Wagner, naturally fascinated by the vigour with which Wagner discussed art."

At this time Berlioz was just forty years old, being ten years Wagner's senior.

CHAPTER IV

1842–1849

Arrives in Dresden – rehearsals of *Rienzi* – success of *Rienzi* –
criticises Mendelssohn – is appointed Court Conductor –
performs Beethoven's Ninth Symphony – Wagner and
Schumann – unreliability of Wagner's autobiography – conducts Weber's *Euryanthe* – pays a visit to Berlin and meets
Liszt – Wagner as conductor – visit of Berlioz – the repertory
under Wagner – his tact and diplomatic powers – prepares
a birthday festival for the King – strange attitude of his
director Lüttichau – composition of *Tannhäuser* – first performance not successful – growing interest in politics –
friendship with Röckel and the revolutionary Bakunin –
revolution in Dresden – arrest of leaders – Wagner escapes
to Weimar.

WAGNER arrived in Dresden on April 26th, 1842,
assisted by a loan from his family through his
brother-in-law Hermann Brockhaus of Leipzig.
The director of the opera house, Lüttichau, and
the conductor, Reissiger, were both, he says, astonished to see him, and his only cordial welcome
was from the chorus-master, Wilhelm Fischer. Of
the two principal singers, Schröder-Devrient was
away, but Tichatschek, who was to play the rôle of
Rienzi, was introduced to his part, and the fact
that he was to have a lot of new costumes and to
appear in one scene glittering in a suit of new silver
armour made him thoroughly enthusiastic. The
summer having arrived, Wagner borrowed more
money and arranged to go to the resort of Töplitz
where he stayed some months and sketched out
the plot of a three-act opera on the mediæval
legend of the Venusberg. Returning to Dresden
to supervise the rehearsals, he heard several

operatic performances, including Grétry's *Blue-beard*; but, as usual, the contrast between his own imagination of what an opera house should be, and of the part he should play in it, contrasted so violently with the comparative meanness of the reality that he was shocked and disgusted. He says he particularly missed the full richness of the strings of the Paris orchestra, and that when opening their new Dresden Opera House they had forgotten to increase these instruments in proportion to the enlarged space. Also the equipment was poor, and generally his impression was such that he declares:

"I actually felt degraded again and nourished within my breast a contempt so deep that for a time I could hardly endure the thought of signing a lasting contract, even with one of the most up-to-date of German opera houses, but sadly wondered what steps I could take to hold my ground between disgust and desire in this strange world."

One might think that Wagner, when he wrote these words, was perhaps attributing to himself at that time feelings which were only developed later, but I doubt if this is so. It is certainly remarkable that a young man of thirty, coming to Dresden to supervise the first production of his own first grand opera after years of obscurity and extreme poverty, should have had such feelings; an almost megalomaniacal craving for splendour is the most characteristic and permanent of Wagner's qualities. I do not believe there has ever existed an artist with less of the artistic love of economy, of achieving great results with small means, than Wagner. The fact that he always insisted on new, most elaborate and splendid scenery for his works; that he was

insatiable in his demands for luxurious costumes
and all incidental paraphernalia; that in his own
home or even in a temporary lodging he craved
for and obtained, however little he could afford it,
rich upholsterings and sumptuous furnishings –
all this indicates a state of mind which is peculiar
to him. It is not accidental or unimportant, it
is fundamental, and, in the world of music, his
own compositions are of a similar nature and perform a similar function to that of his upholstery
and trappings on the stage and in the home. For
Wagner's taste in all these matters was the same.
He loved what was rich, sumptuous, ornate and
elaborate. The beauty of simplicity and economy
did not appeal to him. He never kept anything
in reserve, and whenever he was reticent it was
only diplomacy.

Wagner's diplomatic powers were quite exceptional, nor does he disguise the fact that he used
them unscrupulously to further his own interests,
deceiving all who let themselves be deceived. In
order to get the conductor, Reissiger, to hold
frequent piano rehearsals of *Rienzi* he "had re-
course," he says, "to an ingenious device."
Reissiger was a composer, and he attributed the
ill-success of his own operatic compositions to
indifferent texts and told Wagner that he was
fortunate to have written his own. Wagner's
"device" was to promise to write a libretto for
him, which he did, producing "a page of verse
for every piano rehearsal." This is an example of
Wagner's adaptability, and in its bare outlines is
a story quite creditable to him; but I suspect that
he omits to tell us in what terms he spoke to
Reissiger of his, Reissiger's, abilities as a composer.

It is probable that Reissiger had not known how superior he was to the texts he had set to music until Wagner pointed it out, although Wagner merely says: "I felt bound to confess that he possessed 'a good deal of melody.'" The great enthusiasm of the singer Tichatschek for the part of Rienzi infected the rest of the company, and August and September passed with everybody becoming more and more optimistic and excited, until, in October, the full dress rehearsals produced, says Wagner, "a perfectly intoxicating effect." Wagner and Minna lived "very frugally" in their lodgings on borrowed money until the great day, which turned out to be a real day of deliverance, arrived. Never again was Wagner to have such an experience; he says, "At all the first performances of my works in later days I have been so absorbed by an only too well-founded anxiety as to their success that I could neither enjoy the opera nor form any real estimate of its reception by the public." There was never any doubt about the success of *Rienzi*. The first performance began at six o'clock and lasted until midnight. The third of the five acts was not over until ten o'clock, which was the time at which a normal opera would have concluded. Wagner was in despair: "Thanks to my folly," he says, "I found myself in the unheard-of predicament of being unable to finish an opera, otherwise extremely well received, simply because it was absurdly long. I could only explain the undiminished zeal of the singers and particularly of Tichatschek, who seemed to grow lustier and cheerier the longer it lasted, as an amiable trick to conceal from me the inevitable catastrophe.

But the audience was still there, although it was
past midnight when Wagner finally stood among
the singers, sharing the "thunderous calls of the
audience."

The pronounced success of *Rienzi* was followed
by a fortunate accident, the death of Rastrelli,
the royal director of music; for it was natural
that everybody should think of Wagner as the
most suitable musician for the vacancy. Negotiations were begun, but meanwhile Wagner accompanied Schröder-Devrient to Leipzig, where she
gave a concert including two airs from *Rienzi*
conducted by Wagner and a new overture, the
Ruy Blas by Mendelssohn, who conducted his
own work. Wagner relates this incident with
his characteristic spitefulness, suggesting that
Mendelssohn chose the more operatic *Ruy Blas*
overture instead of his far better *Hebrides*
overture because he was jealous of Wagner's
having had an operatic triumph which he
had never yet had. It is convenient at this
point to mention another reference to Mendelssohn. About a year or so later Mendelssohn was
invited to conduct his *St. Paul* at a Palm Sunday
concert in the Dresden chapel, and Wagner
declares that he was so pleased with the rehearsals of this work that he renewed his former
friendly approach to the composer, but was
quickly disillusioned. The occasion of his dis-
illusionment was the performance of Beethoven's
Eighth Symphony under Reissiger, after the
oratorio. Wagner had noticed that Reissiger at
rehearsal took the *tempo di minuetto* of the third
movement "at a meaningless waltz time," which
resulted in the subsequent trio being made

ridiculous by being played much too fast. On his pointing this out to Reissiger he had promised to observe the proper time, and Wagner mentioned this to Mendelssohn in his box after the conclusion of *St. Paul*, and Mendelssohn had agreed that Wagner was right. The movement began, but Reissiger made the same old mistake, and Wagner was just about to express his indignation when, to his astonishment, Mendelssohn "gave me a friendly nod, as though he thought that this was what I wanted. . . . I was so amazed at this complete absence of feeling on the part of the famous musician that I was struck dumb, and thenceforth my own particular opinion of Mendelssohn gradually matured. . . ."

There is nothing inherently improbable in this story, but we cannot take Wagner's word for it any more than his statement that Robert Schumann supported his "gradually matured" opinion of Mendelssohn. This support was of somewhat later date, when Wagner, now Royal Conductor of the Dresden Opera, prepared and conducted the Ninth Symphony of Beethoven for the Palm Sunday festival of 1846 in Dresden. Wagner himself chose this work against the wishes of the director Lüttichau; but his enthusiasm and conviction overbore all resistance. He says: "If anyone had come upon me unexpectedly while I had the open score before me and had seen me convulsed with sobs and tears as I went through the work in order to consider the best manner of rendering it, he would certainly have asked with astonishment if this were really fitting behaviour for the Conductor Royal of Saxony."

But Wagner, genuinely appreciative and per-
ceptive in a rare degree of Beethoven's great work
as he was, gave such care and attention to every
detail that might help to enlighten the audience
as to the character of the piece, as well as from a
musical point of view preparing the rehearsals,
that the actual performance was possibly the
finest and most successful that had ever yet been
given of this symphony. For example, he says
that he had twelve special rehearsals of the double
basses and 'cellos alone, in order to get the recitative at the beginning of the last movement right –
that is, in a way which sounded "not only perfectly free but which also expressed the most
exquisite tenderness and the greatest energy in a
thoroughly impressive manner." There can be
no doubt that this performance was a revelation
to many musicians. Wagner says that Schumann
looked forward to this performance, as he had
been so disappointed by Mendelssohn's conducting of the work at Leipzig, where he had "quite
misunderstood the time of the first movement";
but he does not tell us what Schumann said, if
anything, after the performance. He says, however, that Gade, who came to hear it from
Leipzig, said he would have gladly paid double
the price of his ticket to hear once again the
recitative by the basses. It is just as well to give
here Wagner's opinion of Robert Schumann. He
heard Schumann conduct his *Paradies und Peri* in
Dresden about this time and says that his "peculiar awkwardness in conducting" stirred his sympathy for the "conscientious musician whose work
made so strong an appeal to me." This sympathy was no doubt stimulated by Schumann's

E

favourable opinion of *Tannhäuser*, expressed
after hearing its production in Dresden at the
end of 1845, when he called on Wagner to tell
him of his approval and of his only objection,
that "the stretto of the second finale was too
abrupt" – which, says Wagner, "proved his
keenness of perception," as Wagner was able to
demonstrate that this abruptness was due to
compulsory cutting of his work. Wagner mixes
up the incidents he relates and the opinions he
expresses so adroitly in *Mein Leben* that one cannot
tell which preceded what. It is only from our
general knowledge of the man and from the
exposure of many distortions and deliberately
misleading statements (about which I shall have
more to say later), through letters and documents
which have come to light since *Mein Leben* was
written, that we know that every statement in
Wagner's own autobiography has to be looked at
suspiciously. He praises those who are useful or
friendly to him; the moment they cease to be of
use or make the slightest fundamental criticism,
they are treated by him with diplomatic cunning
or downright censure and are made to look as
small, unimportant, foolish, or detestable as
possible. So we find that Schumann, after
momentarily gaining his sympathy, soon lost it,
and that Wagner, after appreciating Schumann's
adverse criticism of Mendelssohn, goes on to say
"otherwise his society did not inspire me particularly, and the fact that he was too conservative
to benefit by my views was soon shown, more
especially in his conception of the poem *Genoveva*.
It was clear that my example had only made a
very transient impression on him, only just

enough, in fact, to make him think it advisable to write the text of an opera himself. . . ."

On January 10th, 1843, Wagner gave the usual trial performance necessary for the applicant of Royal Conductor (Hofkapellmeister) to the Court of Saxony, the opera chosen being Weber's *Euryanthe*. It was while one of his rivals for the post was preparing Spontini's *La Vestale* that Wagner went to Berlin to see about the prominent production there of *Rienzi* and the *Holländer*. Nothing was arranged, but, while there, Wagner accidentally met Liszt for the second time. His first meeting in Paris had not been successful. Luckily for him Schröder-Devrient, to whom Wagner had related his unsuccessful meeting with Liszt, was in Berlin also, and she and Wagner were talking about Liszt in her room at her hotel when, says Wagner, "We were startled by hearing from the next room the famous bass part of Donna Anna's 'Revenge' air rapidly executed, in octaves on the piano. 'That's Liszt himself,' she cried. Liszt then entered the room to fetch her for the rehearsal." Schröder-Devrient introduced Wagner to him as the composer of *Rienzi* and a man to whom he had shown the door when he was unknown in Paris. This was quite enough to make the generous Liszt wish to make amends for any discourtesy, however imaginary, he might seem to have been guilty of. The two men became friends and, as we shall see later, Liszt was able to do more for Wagner than any other man.

On February 2nd, 1843, Wagner was officially installed as Hofkapellmeister to the King of Saxony at a salary of 4,500 marks a year, roughly equivalent to £225 or to about four times that

value in our present English currency. This was
an appointment for life, and carried with it a
retiring pension. It meant that Wagner, with
his co-conductor Reissiger, had complete control
of the Dresden Opera House under the general
director or intendant Lüttichau. For a young
musician and composer of thirty years of age
this was an extraordinary piece of good luck,
because the Dresden opera was one of the finest
in Europe, and Dresden and its surroundings
one of the most attractive places in Germany.
He also had the satisfaction of having had his
much loved Weber as a predecessor in the post.
Nevertheless he writes in *Mein Leben* as follows,
after describing the official installation:

"At this polite ceremony it did not escape my
notice that all possibility of future negotiations
over the figure of the salary was cut off; on the
other hand, a substantial exemption in my
favour, the omission of the condition, enforced
even on Weber in his time, of serving a year's
probation under the title of mere musical-director,
was calculated to secure my unconditional
acceptance. My new colleagues congratulated
me, and Lüttichau accompanied me with the
politest phrases to my door, where I fell into the
arms of my poor wife, who was giddy with delight.
Therefore I realised that I must put the best face
I could on the matter, and unless I wished to give
unheard-of offence, I must even congratulate
myself on my appointment as royal conductor."

This is a perfect example of Wagner's way of
misrepresenting events. There is not a word in
Mein Leben of his rivals for the position, Schin-
delmeisser and Gläser; he does not mention the

fact that the candidates each had to prepare an
opera and conduct its performance. Finally
it is stated in Grove that originally Wagner
himself applied for the lesser post of Musikdirek-
tor, with a salary of £180, but that the intendant,
von Lüttichau, obtained for him the better position.

As a conductor Wagner was a great success.
He made many improvements in the seating of
the orchestra, and he made the singers and the
players study completely afresh, with intelligence
and interest, the scores of the regular pieces in
the repertory. Of course he was attacked for his
innovations and energy, but he won friends and
supporters among the more youthful and intelligent people, and he had an enthusiastic
young musician as his official assistant who
believed in him absolutely and was devoted to
him. This was Röckel, a nephew of Hummel,
who applied from Weimar for the post of music-
director under Wagner. Röckel was a fine
pianist and a highly gifted musician; he had
composed an opera, *Farinelli*, which he brought to
Wagner on his arrival at Dresden, but when he
heard Wagner's operas, *Rienzi* and the *Höllander*,
he gave up composition and became one of
Wagner's most fervent and loyal supporters. It
is to him that we are indebted for the information
about the visit of Berlioz to Dresden to which I
have already referred in mentioning the relations
between the two composers. This visit took place
in February 1843 and, according to Grove, the
first of Wagner's official acts was to help Berlioz
in the preparation of the orchestral concerts
Berlioz was to give in Dresden. During Wagner's
six years at Dresden (1843–9) he conducted,

among other less important operas, Weber's
Euryanthe and *Der Freischütz*; Mozart's *Clemenza
di Tito*, *Don Juan*, *Zauberflöte*; Beethoven's
Fidelio; Spohr's *Jessonda*; Marshner's *Hans
Heiling*; Spontini's *La Vestale* and Gluck's *Armida*.
He also gave a special production of Gluck's
Iphigenia in Aulis on February 22nd, 1847, for
which he revised the text, touched up the instru-
mentation and altered the close. This edition was
published and is now generally used.

Wagner was an adept at handling people, and
he always got on well with his singers and musicians. Praeger tells a story that is worth quoting
as an example of Wagner's diplomatic methods.
"On one occasion," he says, "the trombones
were excessively noisy at a *Rienzi* rehearsal, in
the overture, where they should accompany the
violins *piano*. Their braying aroused Wagner's
anger; however, with ready wit . . . turning
good-humouredly to the culprits, he laughingly
said, 'Gentlemen, if I mistake not, we are in
Dresden and not marching round Jericho, where
your ancestors strong of lung blew down the city
walls.' " Not only was he popular with the
members of the orchestra but he won over his
chief, von Lüttichau, and tells an interesting story
which shows Lüttichau's feelings. In the summer
of 1844 the King of Saxony returned from a visit
to England. Wagner thought it would be a good
idea to prepare a special musical reception in
his honour at the King's summer residence in
Pillnitz. As Lüttichau was away he made
arrangements direct with the Lord Chamberlain
and rehearsed a band of instrumentalists and
singers in a reception song of his own composition

(which was the germ of the *Tannhäuser* march).
Everything was arranged when a messenger
arrived, summoning Wagner to the director, who
had just returned to town. "Lüttichau," says
Wagner, "was enraged beyond measure . . . if
his baronial coronet had been on his head during
the interview it would assuredly have tumbled
off." Lüttichau objected to Wagner having gone
direct to the Court officials and also complained
that he was ignoring his colleague Reissiger;
whereupon Wagner offered to hand over his own
composition and the conducting to Reissiger, but
Lüttichau would not have this, says Wagner,
"as he really had an exceedingly poor opinion
of Reissiger, of which I was very well aware."
Nevertheless Reissiger did conduct, and the whole
affair went off most successfully, in the grounds of
Pillnitz, on a beautiful summer day of August
12th, 1844:

"On reaching the castle court we found that
by the Queen's kindly forethought an ample
breakfast had been provided for our party on the
lawn, where the tables were already spread. We
often saw our royal hostess herself, busily super-
vising the attendants or moving with excited
delight about the windows and corridors of the
castle. Every eye beamed rapture to my soul, as
the successul author of the general happiness,
and I almost felt, amid the glories of that day, as
though the millennium had been proclaimed. . . .

"Next morning I was summoned to the presence
of the director. But a change had come over him
during the night. As I began to offer my apologies
for the anxiety I had caused him, the tall thin
man, with the hard dry face, seized me by the

hand and addressed me with a rapturous expression which I am sure no one else ever saw on his face. He told me to say no more about these anxieties. I was a great man, and soon no one would know anything about him, whereas I should be universally admired and loved. . . ."

During 1844 *Tannhäuser* was composed and was first performed at Dresden on October 19th, 1845. It was not a success, and Wagner was very depressed by its comparative failure; but after the second performance it gradually found more favour and was frequently repeated, although it never became as popular as *Rienzi*. In making *Tannhäuser* a comparative success the enthusiasm of men like August Röckel played a large part. Another interesting example of the impression sometimes made by Wagner's personality is to be found in Wagner's account in *Mein Leben* of the evening spent by him with Röckel before the second performance of *Tannhäuser*:

"We met over a glass of beer, and his bright demeanour had such a cheering effect on me that we became very lively. After contemplating my head for some time, he swore that it was impossible to destroy me, that there was something in me, something, probably in my blood, as similar characteristics also appeared in my brother Albert, who was otherwise so unlike me. To speak more plainly, he called it the peculiar *heat* of my temperament. This heat, he thought, might consume others, whereas I appeared to feel at my best when it glowed more fiercely, for he had several times seen me positively ablaze."

During the next few years at Dresden, Wagner went through the experience all original artists

have to go through, of finding himself developing
further and further from the popular taste of the
day. He never repeated his first success with
Rienzi. After that initial triumph each of his new
works found less favour than its predecessor. *Der
Fliegende Holländer* has remained relatively un-
popular to the present time, and, if my opinion
is correct that it is in many ways the best of his
works, this fact is an apt commentary on the superficiality of those who think that the best works of
art are those most people seem to like most.

After the completion of *Tannhäuser* Wagner
wrote in a letter to Carl Gaillard of Berlin: "I
mean to be lazy for a year or so, to make use of
my library and to produce nothing ... if a
dramatic work is to be significant and original it
must result from a step in advance in the life and
culture of the artist; but such a step cannot be
made every few months." Edward Dannreuther
gives some contemporary comments on the reception of *Tannhäuser*: "You are a man of genius,"
said Mme Schröder-Devrient, "but you write
such eccentric stuff it is hardly possible to sing
it"; other comments were: "A distressing,
harassing subject"; "Art ought to be cheerful
and consoling"; "Why should not Tannhäuser
marry Elizabeth?" An interesting fact is that
the story of the pilgrimage to Rome, sung by
Tannhäuser in the third act, which is a masterpiece at its level of dramatic imagination and, if
adequately sung, thrilling in its effect, was
described as pointless and empty and a bore. It
is not surprising that Wagner should have written
of his mood about this time: "A feeling of complete isolation overcame me. It was not my

vanity – I had knowingly deceived myself, and now I felt numbed. I saw a single possibility before me: to induce the public to understand and participate in my aims as an artist."

In this frame of mind it was inevitable that a man of Wagner's impressionability and intelligence should have become interested in the social life in which he as an artist was living and working. His dissatisfaction with his environment and the increasing pressure of his debts, owing to his hopes of royalties from frequent productions in other cities of *Rienzi*, the *Holländer* and *Tannhäuser* not materialising, all combined to make him more and more discontented. The principal critic in Dresden was hostile, and as he was the correspondent of numerous journals in other towns his adverse notices of Wagner's operas had some effect on the outside world. Dannreuther says: "Managers of theatres and German musicians generally took their cue from the journals, and in the end Wagner came to be regarded as an eccentric and unruly personage difficult to deal with. The libretti and scores he submitted were hardly glanced at; in sundry cases, indeed, the parcels were returned unopened." The result was that Wagner took more and more interest in literary and sociological subjects, and in Dresden his friendships and conversations were with men of general rather than musical culture. Also, Wagner met with the usual opposition and lethargy whenever he made any concrete constructive proposal – such, for example, as his plan, prepared in consultation with architects, for replacing some dilapidated old buildings near the theatre with a concert hall. This was rejected and "all my proposals, he says, met with the same success." Any project he prepared had to pass through numerous committee meetings and was liable, even if it survived this process, to be abandoned owing to the objection of some singer or inspector. In short, the struggle between the exceptional individual, with his constructive desires, and the official machinery of social institutions, which is the bulwark of the majority against change and personal ambition, led to Wagner's increasing retirement to a field of activity in which he had more freedom. "I was . . . driven," he says, "to renounce my wasted efforts and, after many a strong discussion and outspoken expression of my sentiments, I withdrew from taking any part whatever in any branch of the management and limited myself entirely to holding rehearsals and conducting performances of the operas provided for me." This left him time to pursue the writing and composition of *Lohengrin*, with which he was occupied during the greater part of 1847. It was during this period also that he re-read the *Nibelung* and *Heldensage* myths, in which he was influenced by the commentaries of the German scholar Mone.

And now we come to Wagner's participation in the revolutionary movement which swept over Europe in the year 1848. "I was sitting in the conductor's desk at a rehearsal of *Martha*," he says, "when, during an interval, Röckel, with the peculiar joy of being in the right, brought me the news of Louis Philippe's flight and the proclamation of the Republic in Paris. This made a strange and almost astonishing impression on me. . . ." In Dresden a *Deutsche Verein* was formed, to press for a constitutional monarchy on a democratic basis. This was the right-wing movement but in opposition to it was a *Vaterlands-Verein*, which was more extreme in its programme and had a republican and socialistic character. Wagner's assistant, August Röckel, became one of the most prominent figures in the latter body. In *Mein Leben*, Wagner, who is concerned (owing to his dependence when it was written upon King Ludwig of Bavaria) to show that his connection with the revolutionary movement was very slight, makes out with his usual adroitness that "everyone who knew him (Röckel) was utterly taken aback at the apparently vital change which had so suddenly taken place in him, when he decided that he had at last found his real vocation – that of an agitator." From Wagner's own description it is clear that Röckel was an absolutely serious and gifted man. For Wagner to describe him as an "agitator" is one of those unpardonable treacheries of which Wagner was so frequently guilty. Wagner says in one place of Röckel: "His persuasive faculties . . . developed in private intercourse into stupefying energy. It was impossible to stop his flow of language with any objection, and those he could not draw over to his cause he cast aside for ever. In his enthusiasm about the problems which occupied his mind day and night, he sharpened his intellect into a weapon capable of demolishing every foolish objection and suddenly stood in our midst like a preacher in the wilderness."

Everything we know about August Röckel shows him to have been a man of strong intelligence and strong character. He was clear-sighted enough to perceive, after meeting Wagner and hearing his early operas, that his own gifts as a musician and composer (although he was a younger man), even if exceptional, were mediocre compared with Wagner's, and he was strong enough to abandon composing altogether and became an ardent and energetic champion of Wagner. The proof of Röckel's influence over Wagner in political matters is Wagner's participation in Röckel's political and sociological activities. At Röckel's request, for example, he read a paper at a meeting of the *Vaterlands-Verein* (a paper which he did not include in his collected works) before some three thousand people, attacking the court sycophants and stating what ought to be the aims of an ideal State and perfect social order. He himself says: "The news of this incredible event spread like wildfire . . . I was congratulated on all sides upon my self-sacrificing audacity." There was a "perfect storm of derision and vituperation" in the Press, and there was a persistent demand from the Court officials that Wagner should be removed from his office. "On this account," says Wagner, "I thought it necessary to write to the monarch personally, in order to explain to him that my action was to be regarded more in the light of a thoughtless indiscretion than as a culpable offence."

The attitude of Wagner is, it seems to me, perfectly clear. He was not only in sympathy with the revolutionary movement and a close friend of several of the leaders, but he took an active part in it although he was more concerned with ideas of cultural development than with politics. The movement in Saxony was a liberal one, and the crisis came in May 1849, on the arbitrary dissolution of the two chambers. The fact that the King of Prussia had offered to the King of Saxony his Prussian soldiers to suppress any possible revolt emphasised the oppression by the autocratic dynasty of the national will and made the revolutionaries patriots or vice versa. According to Praeger, the official records show that at the suppression of the revolt the government indicted "twelve thousand persons . . . including thirty mayors of different towns, about two-thirds of the members of the dissolved chambers, government officials, town councillors, lawyers, clergy, schoolmasters, officers and privates of the army, men of culture, position and social influence." The actual rising in Dresden took place on May 3rd, 1849, when the townspeople, excited by the presence of the soldiers prepared to suppress any demonstration, gathered in groups about the streets, the crowds being more dense near the town hall: "As the crowd swayed, a wooden gate, opening upon a military magazine, gave way. The troops were turned out and defenceless people fired upon – men, women and children dying in the streets. . . ." The result was that barricades were thrown up, some sort of loose organisation was attempted under the leaders Röckel and others, and various tasks were allotted to the members of the "Fatherland-Union," of whom Wagner was one. Wagner was seen by Max von Weber (son of Carl Maria von Weber) carrying a musket; he himself declared, in a letter to Eduard Röckel, dated March 1851: "I was present everywhere, actually superintending the bringing in of convoys," and he only by accident escaped being arrested with Röckel. A note from Wagner was found on Röckel in which occurs the following phrase: "return immediately; a premature outbreak is feared." One fact must not be omitted which also had its effect in stimulating Wagner's revolutionary activities, and that is the cancellation of the production of *Lohengrin* owing to the hostility of the Court. On the arrest of the leaders Röckel, Heubner, Bakunin and others, Wagner very wisely fled, as he saw that the rising was a failure. He had his future as a composer to think of, also his manuscript of the completed *Lohengrin*. He fled to Liszt at Weimar, where he stayed several days. They learned that a warrant for his arrest had been issued, and Liszt helped him to escape through Bavaria, by means of a borrowed passport, into Switzerland, and he arrived at Zurich on the last day of May 1849.

Röckel, Heubner and Bakunin were imprisoned and brought before a regular tribunal in January 1850, when they were sentenced to death. A second trial, owing to the popular clamour, was conceded to them on April 16th, 1850, but it confirmed the previous sentence. This, however, was commuted to imprisonment by the King of Saxony who was averse to capital punishment. There is not the slightest doubt that Wagner, if caught, would have received the same sentence. He was regarded in exactly the same light as Röckel, and he had been intimately associated with both Röckel and the Russian revolutionary Bakunin. In spite of the fact that he skilfully minimised his political activities when writing *Mein Leben*, the account of Bakunin he gives there is sufficiently sympathetic to reveal a fairly close association. He met him through Röckel, and says: "I was immediately struck by his singular

and altogether imposing personality . . . it was
impossible to triumph over his opinions, stated as
they were with the utmost conviction, and over-
stepping in every direction even the extremest
bounds of radicalism . . . he argued that all
that was necessary to set in motion a world-wide
movement was to convince the Russian peasant,
in whom the natural goodness of oppressed human
nature had preserved the most child-like characteristics, that it was perfectly right and well pleasing to God for them 'to burn their lords' castles,
with everything in and about them.' . . . In spite
of their republic and their socialism à la Proudhon
he thought nothing of the French, and as for the
Germans, he never mentioned them to me.
Democracy, republicanism and anything else of
the kind he regarded as unworthy of consideration . . . he used to puzzle any who professed
their readiness for self-sacrifice by telling them
that it was not the so-called tyrants who were so
obnoxious but the smug Philistines. As a type of
these he pointed to a Protestant parson and
declared that he would not believe he had really
reached the full stature of a man until he saw him
commit his own parsonage, with his wife and
child, to the flames. . . . Even while he was
preaching these horrible doctrines, Bakunin,
noticing that my eyes troubled me, shielded them
with his outstretched hand from the naked light
for a full hour, in spite of my protestations. . . .
The annihilation of all civilisation was the goal
upon which his heart was set."

One story Wagner tells is worth relating.
Wagner described to Bakunin his own ideas of an
artistic revolution. "I had just then," he says,

"been inspired by a study of the Gospels to conceive the plan of a tragedy for the ideal stage of the future, entitled 'Jesus of Nazareth.' Bakunin begged me to spare him any details; and when I sought to win him over to my project by a few verbal hints, he wished me luck but insisted that I must at all costs make Jesus appear as a weak character. As for the music of the piece, he advised me, amid all the variations, to use only one set of phrases, namely: for the tenor, 'Off with his head!'; for the soprano, 'Hang him!'; and for the basso continuo, 'Fire! fire!' And yet I felt more sympathetically drawn to this prodigy of a man when I one day induced him to hear me play and sing the first scenes of my *Fliegende Holländer*. After listening with more attention than most people gave, he exclaimed, during a momentary pause, 'That is stupendously fine!' and wanted to hear more."

Here I may conclude the story of Röckel's imprisonment and Wagner's enforced exile, owing to their share in the 1848–9 revolutionary movement. After thirteen years of imprisonment, that is from 1849 to 1862, August Röckel was unconditionally released. He could have obtained his freedom earlier if he had been willing to make a declaration of error and had begged forgiveness for his political sins. Others did this and were released, but Röckel was made of different stuff, and, in the end, the Saxon government found it so intolerable to be forced to keep this man in prison that he was given his freedom. Wagner, on the other hand, during his thirteen years of exile, used all the influence he could bring to bear to get an amnesty and the right to re-enter his

F

native country. He wrote the most abject letters expressing sorrow and regret for his misdeeds to the King of Saxony, letters which make one blush for Wagner and which in justice to Wagner it must be said that even he found some difficulty in writing; but it was all in vain, and his exile lasted as long as Röckel's imprisonment.

It is pleasant to make a moral judgment on Wagner's behaviour in this matter, but it is a pleasure that a fine palate will reject. Let us rather admire the integrity of Röckel *and* the integrity of Wagner. Each was true to himself. Röckel was a sincere, gifted and honest man, and Wagner was a sincere, gifted and honest actor, in the revolutionary movement. Röckel believed in what he said and did in this cause; Wagner played the rôle with a good actor's sympathy; but his heart was elsewhere, and has it not been said that where one's heart is there will one's treasure be also?

CHAPTER V

1849–1861

In October 1849 Wagner became a citizen of
Zurich, where he was joined by his wife Minna,
his dog Peps, his parrot Papo, and his wife's
reputed sister Nathalie. Minna had succeeded in
selling the furniture of their Dresden home
advantageously and brought to Zurich a sum of
about three hundred francs, with a few of their
belongings, including a Breitkopf and Härtel
grand pianoforte which "looked better than it
sounded."

Wagner did not look upon his situation in the
same light as Minna, for whom it was a disaster.
He declares that at times his spirits rose "to a

level of freedom and comfort that I had never enjoyed before," and, apart from his concern about
his precarious financial situation, he was probably
delighted to be rid of his official position and all
the duties it imposed upon him. The complete
freedom and leisure he now enjoyed bore immediate fruit, for he began to think about his
artistic ideas and, after having received some
money from the generous Liszt at Weimar, he
became so elated that he says: "The extraordinary birdlike freedom of my existence had
the effect of exciting me more and more. I was
often frightened at the excessive outbursts of exaltation to which I was prone." In this state he
began to write out his ideas, thinking he might
also earn some money by his pen. His first essay
was entitled *Die Kunst und die Revolution* ("Art and
Revolution") for which he was quite well paid by
Otto Wigand of Leipzig, who published it as a
pamphlet, and it was successful enough to go into a
second edition. He then began to write *Das Kunst-
werk der Zukunft* ("The Art-work of the Future")
and spent most of his time reading and writing.
The mother of his friend Ritter sent him a sum of
fifteen hundred marks, and he also received a sympathetic letter from young Mme Laussot, who had
called on him in Dresden. His comment on
these two events is: "These were the first signs
of that new phase in my life upon which I entered
from this day forth, and in which I accustomed
myself to look upon the outward circumstances of
my existence as being merely subservient to my
will. And by this means I was able to escape
from the hampering narrowness of my home
life."

Having some money at his disposal, he was urged by Minna to go to Paris to try to get some of his operas produced there. He had no belief in such a project, but Minna was insistent, and he left for Paris in February 1850. "I was filled with the most extraordinary feelings," he said, "but the spark of hope which was then kindled in my breast certainly had nothing whatever to do with the belief that had been imposed on me from without, that I was to make a success in Paris as a composer of operas."

What was this "spark of hope" to which he so cryptically refers? Possibly it was Jessie Laussot, who with Karl Ritter had called on him in Dresden full of enthusiasm over *Tannhäuser*. She was an Englishwoman, a Miss Taylor, married to a young French merchant named Laussot living in Bordeaux. While he was in Paris he received a communication from Frau Julie Ritter, the mother of his friend Karl Ritter, offering him, in conjunction with Mme Laussot, an annual pension, so that he could devote himself to his creative work. He was invited to Bordeaux where he went in March 1850, only too delighted to leave Paris since he shared none of Minna's illusions as to the possibility of his operas being performed there. But he had to make Minna understand the reasons for abandoning the Paris project, and he wrote to her as artfully as possible:

"Nobody," he says, "could have behaved more kindly, delicately and nobly than our friend Mme Laussot. I should have thought, my love, that you would be really proud to see the deep impression which your husband's works can make on healthy, unperverted, noble hearts, and the demonstration of unselfish devotion and sympathy which he is able to call forth. Can you honestly bring yourself to look down upon such a proof of my artistic success – for it is my art alone which has brought this about – or actually to rate it lower than the so-called brilliant successes which are achieved with the foolish, slovenly, heartless men of our opera-going public by means of speculation and trickery? . . . Supposing we treat these people with contempt and think only of money. Very well, here is money, as much of it as we need for a quiet and even comfortable existence; and it has not been won by speculation from a trumpery crowd, but has been handed to me in the most delicate manner by a noble-hearted person, from sheer joy in the works that I had created out of my inmost self."

This letter is more than plausible, it is irrefutable by any argument; nevertheless it is pure humbug. Jessie Laussot was in love with Wagner, and he (not unnaturally, seeing that she was twenty-two years of age, pretty, attractive and clever) with her; but Wagner was in a situation where all explanations are a betrayal, no matter to whichever of the two parties they may be made. He might have said to Minna: "You are my wife, you must trust in my affection for you and ask no question"; and to Jessie Laussot: "I love you and will accept your help"; but not only was such an attitude contrary to his idealising, histrionic temperament, it was probably too difficult to sustain. The risk that each might refuse to play the rôle allotted to her and that he might be left without either of them was too great for the comfort-loving Wagner, for to him some loving and self-sacrificing woman was absolutely indispensable. He took the diplomatic course and so laid himself open to counter-diplomacy on the part of Jessie's husband and mother. While Wagner was temporising and explaining, they were busy persuading Jessie that Wagner was not in love with her but only exploiting her. The result was that Jessie ultimately refused to see Wagner or open his letters (it is said by Dr. Julius Knapp that her husband and mother kept some of his letters, and also a second journey he made to Bordeaux to see her, secret from her). This caused Wagner to write a series of characteristic explanations to Frau Julie Ritter, in which all the blame is put upon Jessie Laussot!

"From the way in which things were going," he writes, "I was already beginning to think that Jessie had undertaken something beyond her strength and was not equal to carrying out her plan. Not for a moment was I blind to the fact that it would require a revolutionary force of character to go through with it or that her resolve and her feeling must be their own justification; and that further, such justification could only exist if the strength of these proved so invincible as to render any and every consideration feeble and useless by contrast. Let anyone show himself a love-rebel – even if it means his ruin – and he is mine; and in the case of this love being personal to me I should wish for nothing better than to crash with him. In this light and no other did I regard my relation with Jessie after she had told me of her resolve, and from this point of view only could feel able to put aside all considerations no matter how painful, on my own side. . . . Only

Jessie could help Jessie, and that solely by presenting an unshaken front to the wiles and intrigues with which those around her very naturally sought to alienate her from me. And now the only power that could help her – the power of love – has been rejected and betrayed. She has lost her true self – for she is weak! The woman who was to have brought me salvation has proved herself a child! Forgive me if I can only regard her as pitiable. . . ."

I wish I could have quoted the whole of this extraordinary document but I have given enough to show its character. The ordinary philistine will, of course, dismiss the letter as contemptible; but, as always with Wagner, there is much more to be said. We have no reason to doubt that Wagner believed what he wrote. He did need a woman with sufficient force of character to sacrifice everything for him, and he first of all found one in Minna and later on another one in Cosima Liszt, who married Hans von Bülow and had the will and strength to abandon the loyal and decent Hans for Wagner. But what is sufficiently obvious is the superficiality of Wagner's feeling for Jessie. In Wagner's relations with women he shows his real nature just as much as he shows it in his music. We may go further and say that in the man and the musician the same qualities are discernible, and that in the end we may come to doubt whether there is anything in Wagner's music but Wagner.

Wagner's relations with women may be described as fairly normal. He was easily susceptible, and at every period of his career, from his university days to the end of his life (when he died of a heart attack brought on, it is said, by a quarrel with Cosima about including a certain young singer in the cast at Bayreuth), he was nearly always involved in some love intrigue. A specimen of these miscellaneous and unimportant affairs is to be found in an episode of his later life, in 1843, when he engaged the daughter of a Vienna pork-butcher to look after him. He and his wife Minna were then living apart owing to her bad health and their quarrels over Mathilde Wesendonck, who by this time was living again with her husband from whom she had been alienated on Wagner's account. Wagner left this young daughter of the pork-butcher in charge of his house in Vienna while he was away on a series of concert tours, and there exists a letter he wrote to her which is to be quoted for the revelation it makes of Wagner's nature. It is as follows:

"DEAR MARIECHEN, – Next Monday I am coming home again. Shall arrive in Vienna at half-past seven in the evening at the North Station. Let Franz be there punctually with the carriage and have everything ready for my trunk too. And so, sweetheart, make the house look really nice so that I can rest in comfort again as I long to do. Everything is to be thoroughly clean and well heated. Be sure you prepare my pretty work-room properly for me. When the stove is lighted, open the door wide so that the temperature of the room is warm. *Perfume it too; buy the best scents so that it may be really fragrant.* How I look forward to resting there again with you. (The pink drawers are ready, I hope? ? ?)

"Yes, yes, be very pretty and charming. *I deserve to have a really good time again.* At Christmas I shall light the tree and there will be presents for all, including you, sweetheart. You need not *tell* everyone of my arrival. Only let Franz order the barber and hairdresser for Thursday morning at half-past eight. Till Wednesday then; half-past seven in Vienna and at Penzing shortly after. I leave it entirely to you whether you meet me at the station. Perhaps it is nicer if you greet me at home in the warm rooms. I shall only want the coupé, I expect. Remember me to Franz and Anna. They are to make everything very nice. Many kisses to my sweetheart. *Auf wiedersehen!*

"R. WAGNER."

No doubt this letter is more characteristic of the Wagner of 1863 than of the Wagner of 1850, but his letter to Frau Wille about Jessie Laussot is also an example of Wagner's resilience and self-protectiveness. With the failure of Jessie Laussot it was all the more necessary to appease Minna. He sent Karl Ritter to Zurich to explain matters to her, and when Ritter returned telling him that Minna had prepared a new house by the lake for them, he wrote to her, explaining away the Laussot affair. This was one of the rare occasions when Wagner's prowess in explanation failed. His letter to Minna is in the Burrell Collection (unpublished), and Minna's remark upon it is simply: "Our reunion had nothing whatever to do with this idiotic letter." The contrast between Minna and Wagner is often brilliantly lighted up by some such brief comment of

Minna's. For example there exists in the Burrell Collection a letter, dated April 7th, 1850, from Jessie Laussot to Minna, across which Minna has simply written: "False devastating creature!" The fact that Wagner never abandoned Minna is not surprising; her charm, good looks and intelligence were supported by a character that was as completely non-bogus as Wagner's was completely bogus. But it becomes more and more clear when studying his life that being bogus through and through, being a profound humbug, a humbug to the very bottom of himself without reservation, without the faintest shadow of self-doubting, he becomes, as it were, completely genuine. You can turn him inside out and he is everywhere the same, completely of a piece, having an integrity such as few men possess, the integrity of his genius, which is essentially a genius for fraud – brilliant, incomparable and to many people, enchanting, fraud.

Two extracts from letters he wrote at the time will show Wagner's state of mind after this, the first of a series of crises in his personal life. The following refers to Jessie Laussot:

"But no, we will not revile her, this dead – murdered – woman, for she was Love. Never shall I be ashamed of this love: even though it fade away and I become convinced that nothing can revive it, her kiss remains the richest enjoyment of my life. Neither honour, nor splendour, nor fame could turn the scale against it. Farewell dear lovely departed one! You were precious to me above everything, and never will I forget you. Farewell!"

The other extract refers to Minna:

"Poor woman, she was so rich, had so much to give! How many a man she might have made perfectly happy! Alas, that you lacked just the one thing, the one without which all love is a deception, all tenderness a martyrdom, all union a torture: the power to understand him whom you think you love, the understanding whence comes that joy in the beloved which alone enables us to be joyful in all our sufferings. I had to part from you in order to love you again. I had to do it even if it meant the end of us both."

The strange thing is that these extracts are both true – for Wagner. And if they are true for him any outside comment must take this fact into account. Minna did not fully understand Wagner. She thought she would have been more contented if he had been a prosperous mediocrity. But she would not have felt the same towards a prosperous mediocrity, and that she did not fully realise. There was a real conflict between them at times, and we may see this from Wagner's letter to Uhlig, shortly after his return to Minna in Zurich, in July 1850, when he wrote:

"I have got a new wife, although she is the same as ever in everything. I now know at least that – whatever may happen to me– she will stand by me until death. I for my part had honestly no idea of, so to say, testing her: but as things have turned out she has been through a fiery ordeal such as all must overcome who, in these days, decide with open eyes to cast in their lot with those who see the future and steer straight for it."

Wagner settled down with Minna in her new quarters at Zurich on the second floor of an inn

called "Zum Abendstern" overlooking the lake.
In August he and Minna went for a tour and
climbed the Rigi, during which he says his wife
showed symptoms of heart trouble. They spent
the evening of August 28th, 1850, at the Schwan
Inn in Lucerne, while the first performance of
Lohengrin was taking place in Weimar under
Liszt's direction, watching the clock and calculat-
ing the different stages of the performance. The
reception of *Lohengrin* was mixed, but it made a
deep impression on some musicians, and Liszt
persisted in his advocacy of Wagner's music,
writing an account of the production of
Lohengrin in French which Karl Ritter translated
into German. This was published in the
Illustrierte Zeitung, and a similar treatise on
Tannhäuser was written by Liszt which also had
the effect of increasing Wagner's reputation.

During the winter of 1850 Wagner wrote his
prose work *Oper und Drama* and obtained a position
as music director at the theatre for his young
friend Karl Ritter (who had been a talented
pupil of Robert Schumann), guaranteeing his
capacity by undertaking to perform his duties if
necessary. For the opening opera Weber's *Der
Freischütz* was chosen, and Wagner relates how he
was amazed, when Karl Ritter started to go
through the score with him on the pianoforte, to
discover that Ritter had "no idea of accompani-
ment. He played the arrangement for the pianoforte with the characteristic carelessness of an
amateur who attaches no importance to lengthen-
ing a bar by incorrect fingering. He knew
nothing whatever about rhythmic precision or
tempo, the very essentials of a conductor's career.

I felt completely nonplussed and was absolutely at a loss what to say."

Wagner had to take Ritter's place for the first performance of *Der Freischütz* and he realised that Ritter could not possibly fill the position of musical-director alone. Fortunately an event occurred which solved the difficulty and introduced to Wagner a man who, later on, was to play an intimate and important part in his life, namely, Hans von Bülow. The father of Hans wanted his son to enter the civil or the diplomatic service, and Hans wrote a despairing letter to Wagner, who sent a reply by Karl Ritter to Hans at his father's house at Lake Constance, telling him that if he felt an overwhelming impulse to be a musician and was prepared to endure every hardship he, Wagner, would help him. Ritter gave the letter to young von Bülow, who decided to go at once with him to Zurich, where they arrived the next day. Wagner arranged that Bülow was to share Ritter's contract at the theatre, and Bülow immediately showed how exceptional his talents were on the first occasion he had to take the conductor's baton. He also made an immense impression on Wagner by his brilliant playing of Liszt's difficult arrangement for the pianoforte of the *Tannhäuser* overture.

By 1853 Wagner had written the whole of the poem of the "Ring des Nibelungen" but he had not composed a note of music since he had fled to Switzerland from Dresden. The poem of the "Ring" was read aloud by him at different times to several parties of his friends, and in July 1853 he planned a journey to Italy, as a means of putting him in a favourable mood for the task of

composing the music to his huge tetralogy. He
had made the acquaintance in Zurich of a wealthy
young silk merchant and his wife, Otto and
Mathilde Wesendonck, who had attended some
of the concerts conducted by him there, and it
was Wesendonck who gave him the money to
make a trip to Italy. His own account of what
happened is so interesting that I will quote it
in full:

"At last, in the month of September, which I
had been told was quite suitable for visiting Italy,
I set off on the journey, via Geneva, full of
indescribable ideas of what was before me and of
what I might see as the outcome of my search.
Once again amid all kinds of strange adventures
I reached Turin by special mail coach over Mont
Cenis. Finding nothing to detain me there more
than a couple of days, I hurried on to Genoa.
There, at any rate, the longed-for marvels seemed
to be within reach. The grand impression produced on me by that city overcomes, even to this
day, any longing to visit the rest of Italy. For a
few days I was in a dream of delight; but my
extreme loneliness amidst all these impressions
soon made me feel that I was a stranger in that
world, and that I should never be at home
in it.

"Absolutely inexperienced as I was in searching
out the treasures of art on a systematic plan, I
gave myself up in this new world to a peculiar
state of mind that might be described as a musical
one, and my main idea was to find some turning
point that might induce me to remain there in
quiet enjoyment. My only object still was to find
a refuge where I might enjoy the congenial peace

suited to some new artistic creation. In consequence, however, of thoughtlessly indulging in
ices, I soon got an attack of dysentery which produced the most depressing lassitude after my
previous exaltation. I wanted to flee from the
tremendous noise of the harbour, near which I
was staying, and seek for the most absolute calm;
and, thinking a trip to Spezia would benefit me,
I went there by steamer a week later. Even this
excursion, which lasted only one night, was
turned into a trying adventure, thanks to a violent
head wind. The dysentery became worse owing
to seasickness, and, in the most utterly exhausted
condition, scarcely able to drag myself another
step, I made for the best hotel in Spezia, which,
to my horror, was situated in a noisy narrow
street.

"After a night spent in fever and sleeplessness,
I forced myself to take a long tramp the next day
through the hilly country, which was covered with
pine woods. It all looked dreary and desolate,
and I could not think what I should do there.
Returning in the afternoon I stretched myself,
dead tired, on a hard couch, awaiting the long
desired hour of sleep. It did not come; but I
fell into a kind of somnolent state in which I
suddenly felt as though I were sinking in swiftly
flowing water. The rushing sound formed itself
in my brain into a musical sound, the chord of
E flat major, which continually re-echoed in
broken forms; these broken chords seemed to be
melodic passages of increasing motion, yet the
pure triad of E flat major never changed, but
seemed by its continuance to impart infinite
significance to the element in which I was

sinking. I awoke in sudden terror from my doze, feeling as though the waves were rushing high over my head. I at once recognised that the orchestral overture to the *Rheingold*, which must long have been latent within me, though it had been unable to find definite form, had at last been revealed to me. I then quickly realised my own nature; the stream of life was not to flow to me from without but from within. I decided to return to Zurich immediately and begin the composition of my great poem. I telegraphed to my wife to let her know my decision, and to have my study in readiness."

It has always seemed to me that this is one of the most interesting accounts of the way a musical composition comes into being, and it adds to the completeness of this illustration when one knows that Wagner was not able to start straight away on the composition of *Rheingold*, having an appointment with Liszt in Bâle at the beginning of October. He travelled with Liszt to Paris, where he read to Liszt's friends the whole poem of the "Ring des Nibelungen," and there he met Liszt's three children, Blandine, Cosima and Daniel. At the end of October he left Paris and returned to Zurich, and, in his lodgings at the beginning of November 1853, he began to compose the music to *Rheingold*, after an interval of five and a half years (since March 1848) during which he had not written a note of music. He himself remarks:

"As I soon found myself in the right mood for composing, this return to my work can best be compared to a reincarnation of my soul after it had been wandering in other spheres. As far

G

as the technique was concerned, I soon found myself in a difficulty when I started to write down the orchestral overture, conceived in Spezia in a kind of half-dream, in my usual way of sketching it out on two lines. I was compelled to resort to the complete score-formula; this tempted me to try a new way of sketching, which was a very hasty and superficial one, from which I immediately wrote out the complete score. This process often led to difficulties, as the slightest interruption in my work made me lose the thread of my rough draft, and I had to start from the beginning before I could recall it to my memory.

"I did not let this occur in regard to *Rheingold*. The whole of this composition had been finished in outline on the 16th of January, 1854, and consequently the plan for the musical structure of this work in four parts had been drawn in all its thematic proportions, as it was in this great prelude that these thematic foundations of the whole had to be laid.

"I remember how much my health improved during the writing of this work; and my surroundings during that time consequently left very little impression on my mind."

One might conclude from the above extracts that the full score of *Rheingold* was completed by January 16th, 1854, but this is not the case. Wagner's method of writing down his music was evidently to compose what may be described as a vocal outline in full score and then to instrument it fully afterwards. Possibly in his first full sketch he would jot down hints of instrumentation; but it is part of the nature of creative genius to be able to carry in the mind an almost infinite mass of relationships in suspension, as it were, ready for precipitation at the right moment. So we find Wagner writing in his autobiography, a few paragraphs later than the extract I have just quoted, as follows:

"During the first months of the new year (1854) I also conducted a few orchestral concerts. To please my friend Sulzer I produced, amongst other works, the overture to Gluck's *Iphigenia in Aulis*, after having written a new finale to it. The necessity of altering the finale by Mozart induced me to write an article for the Brendel musical journal on this artistic problem. These occupations did not, however, prevent me from working at the *Rheingold* score, which I quickly jotted down in pencil on a few single sheets. On the 28th of May I finished the instrumentation of the *Rheingold*."

At this point it is convenient to refer to the time taken by the composition of the music of the four sections of the "Ring" as a whole. We see that the first part *Das Rheingold* was composed between November 1853 and May 1854, the fundamental musical idea of the Prelude (which is, essentially, the music of the Rhine and the Rhine-maidens) having come into Wagner's mind in Spezia in September 1853. I will now tabulate in a convenient form the times of composition of the whole work from the beginning:

Time	Place	Work
September 1853	Spezia ..	The E flat major Prelude to *Rheingold*
November 1853–Jan. 1854 ..	Zurich ..	The first full draft of *Das Rheingold*

Time	Place	Work
January–May 28th, 1854 ..	Zurich ..	The instrumenta-tion of *Das Rhein-gold*
May–July 1854	,, ..	The first draft of the 1st Scene of *Die Walküre*
End of July–August 1854 ..	,, ..	Completion of 1st Act of *Die Walküre*
August–September 1854 ..	,, ..	First fair copy of the full score of *Das Rheingold* made

I will interrupt the table at this point to remark
that it was somewhere about this time that
Wagner came across and read for the first time
Schopenhauer's *Die Welt als Wille und Vorstellung*
(The World as Will and Imagination). He himself
says: "For many years afterwards that book
never left me, and by the summer of the following
year I had already studied the whole of it for the
fourth time. The effect thus gradually wrought
upon me was so extraordinary and certainly
exerted a decisive influence on the whole course of
my life ... I was prompted to send the vener-
ated philosopher a copy of my Nibelungen poem.
To its title I merely added by hand the words,
"With reverence," but without writing a single
word to Schopenhauer himself. ... In addition
to these studies I continued writing the music to
the *Walküre*. I was living in great retirement all
this time, my sole relaxation being to take long
walks in the neighbourhood, and, as usual with
me when hard at work at my music, I felt the
longing to express myself in poetry. This must
have been partly due to the serious mood created
by Schopenhauer, which was trying to find

ecstatic expression. It was some such mood that inspired the conception of a *Tristan und Isolde*."

Time	Place	Work
September–December 1854 ..	Zurich ..	First sketch of the 2nd and 3rd Acts of *Die Walküre*
January 1855	,, ..	Beginning of instrumentation of *Die Walküre*

Here there was an interruption due to Wagner's being invited to conduct for the Philharmonic Society in London. He left for London on February 26th, but his activities there did not wholly stop him from composing, in spite of what he describes as "uninterrupted ill-health . . . caused no doubt by the state of the London climate at that season of the year which is notorious all over the world. . . . For one thing I could not get my house sufficiently warmed through, and the work that I had brought with me was the first thing to suffer. The instrumentation of the *Walküre*, which I had hoped to finish off here, only advanced by a paltry hundred pages. I was hindered in this principally by the circumstance that the sketches from which I had to work on the instrumentation had been written down without considering the extent to which a prolonged interruption of my working humour might affect the coherence of the sketch. How often did I sit before those pencilled pages as if they had been unfamiliar hieroglyphics which I was incapable of deciphering! In absolute despair I plunged into Dante, making for the first time a serious effort to read him. The *Inferno*, indeed, became a never-to-be-forgotten reality in that London atmosphere.

"But at last came the hour of deliverance. . . .
I hurried home by way of Paris, which was
clothed in its summer glory, saw people really
promenading again, instead of pushing through
the streets on business. And so I returned to
Zurich full of cheerful impressions on the 30th
June, my net profits being exactly one thousand
francs."

Time	Place	Work
February–June 1855	.. London ..	Instrumentation of *Die Walküre*
August 1855–March 1856	.. Zurich ..	First fair copy of *Die Walküre* completed

"By this time illness and the stress of work,"
says Wagner, "had reduced me to a state of
unusual irritability, and I can remember how
extremely bad-tempered I was when our friends
the Wesendoncks came in the evening to pay a
sort of congratulatory visit on the completion of
my score. I expressed my opinion of this way of
sympathising with my work with such extraordinary bitterness that the poor insulted visitors
departed abruptly in great consternation, and it
took many explanations, which I had great
difficulty in making, to atone for the insult as the
days went on. My wife came out splendidly on
this occasion in her efforts to smooth things
over."

Wagner spent two months of the summer of
1856 taking a hydropathic cure and then began
sketching the composition of *Siegfried* on September 22nd, 1856. He gives the following amusing
account of this:

"A tinker had established himself opposite my
house and stunned my ears all day long with his

incessant hammering. In my disgust at never being able to find a detached house protected from any kind of noise I was on the point of deciding to give up composing altogether until the time when this indispensable condition should be fulfilled. But it was precisely my rage over the tinker that, in a moment of agitation, gave me the theme for Siegfried's furious outburst against the bungling Mime. I played over the childishly quarrelsome Polter theme in G minor to my sister, furiously singing the words at the same time, which made us all laugh so much that I decided to make one more effort. This resulted in my writing down a good part of the first scene by the time Liszt arrived on the 13th October."

Wagner gives an interesting account of Liszt's visit. Liszt had finished his "Faust" and "Dante" symphonies and played them to Wagner on the pianoforte. His symphonic poems "Orpheus" and "Les Preludes" were performed by the orchestra of the St. Gall musical society, conducted by Liszt, and Wagner conducted Beethoven's "Eroïca" symphony. "My conception and rendering of Beethoven's work," says Wagner, "made a powerful impression upon Liszt, whose opinion was the only one which had any real weight with me." On Liszt's departure Wagner returned to his work and completed the first act of *Siegfried*, "writing down the composition in full to take the place of the earlier rough pencil draft," and immediately set to work on the orchestration.

Time	Place	Work
January–February 1857 ..	Zurich ..	1st Act of *Siegfried* completed
February–August 1857 ..	Zurich (Asyl)	2nd Act of *Siegfried*

At this point the composition of the "Ring des Nibelungen" was interrupted for what turned out to be a period of twelve years. It was not until 1869 that Wagner was able to return to the composition of *Siegfried*. From that time he worked steadily and the "Ring" was completed as follows:

Time			Place		Work
1869	..	..	Triebschen	..	3rd Act of *Siegfried*
1870	..	..	,,	..	Vorspiel and 1st Act of *Götterdämerung*
1872–4	..	..	Bayreuth	..	Full score of *Götterdämmerung* completed

As we have seen, the composition of the music to *Die Walküre* was partially interrupted by Wagner's visit to London in 1855. This was his second visit to England, and it came about in this way. Ferdinand Praeger, the friend of August Röckel, was living in London and was an intimate friend of Professor Sainton, an eminent violinist of French origin who was the leader of the orchestra and one of the directors of the Royal Philharmonic Society. Praeger did not know Wagner at that time, and his opinions were merely the reflections of Röckel's; but it appears that Sainton had heard Wagner conduct in Dresden, and together they persuaded the Philharmonic Society to engage Wagner for a season. Praeger contributed an article to the *New York Musical Gazette* dated February 24th, 1855, the following extract from which will explain the whole circumstances:

"The musical public of London is in a state of excitement which cannot be described. Costa, the autocrat of London conductors, is just now writing an oratorio and no longer cares for, what he would have sacrificed anything before he got possession of it, namely, the conductorship of the Old Philharmonic; and whom to have in his place has for some time sorely puzzled the directors of the said society. No Englishman would do, that is certain, for the orchestra adores Costa; and besides, it belongs to Covent Garden, where Costa reigns supreme (and where he really does wonders; being musical conductor and stage-manager . . .). Whom to seek for, the government knew not. They made overtures to Berlioz, but he had already signed an engagement with the New Philharmonic, their presumptuous and hated rival. Things looked serious, appalling, to the Old Philharmonic: they were in danger of losing many subscribers, and a strong tide was setting in against them. At last, seeing themselves on the verge of dissolution and the New Philharmonic ready to act as pall-bearers, they resolved upon a risk-all, life or death remedy: Richard Wagner was engaged! Yes, this red republican of music is to preside over the Old Philharmonic of London, the most classical, orthodox and exclusive society on the globe. . . .

"To see Wagner and Berlioz, the most ultra red republicans existing in music, occupying the two most prominent positions in the musical world of this classical, staid, proper, exclusive, conservative London, is an unmitigatedly 'stunning' fact. . . ."

We can see that Praeger was an excellent journalist, and it is amusing to turn to Wagner's comment on his enthusiastic herald when he meets him in London. "Arriving in London on 2nd March, I first went to see Ferdinand Praeger.

In his youth he had been a friend of the Röckel
brothers, who had given me a very favourable
account of him. He proved to be an unusually
good-natured fellow, though of an excitability
insufficiently balanced by his standard of culture.
After spending the first night at his house, I installed myself the following day with his help in
a house in Portland Terrace, in the neighbourhood
of Regent's Park, of which I had agreeable re-
collections from former visits. I promised myself
a pleasant stay there in the coming spring, if only
on account of its close proximity to that part of
the park where beautiful copper beeches over-
shadowed the path. But though I spent four
months in London it seemed to me that spring
never came, the foggy climate so overclouded all
the impressions I received."

Wagner conducted eight concerts for the Philharmonic Society and his programmes included
all the Beethoven symphonies except the first and
second, Mozart's symphonies in E flat and C, and
works by Spohr, Mendelssohn and Weber. Of
his own works he conducted the overture to *Tannhäuser* (twice) and the Introduction, Bridal Pro-
cession, Wedding Music and Epithalamium from
Lohengrin. The Press on the whole was hostile,
but he made a good impression on the more
intelligent musicians. After the first concert,
Praeger, Sainton, Lüders, Karl Klindworth and
Wagner had supper together. Praeger says:

"His volubility at the table knew no bounds.
Anecdotes and reminiscences of his early life
poured forth with a freshness, a vigour and spark-
ling vivacity just like some mountain cataract
leaping impetuously forward. He spoke with

evident pleasure of his reception by the audience; praised the orchestra, remarking how faithfully they had borne in mind and reproduced the impressions he had sought to give them at the rehearsal. On this point he was only regretful that the inspiration, the divination, the artistic electricity, as it were, which is in the air among German or French executants, should be wanting here; or, as he phrased it, 'ils jouent parfaite- ment, mais le feu sacré leur manque.'

"Then follows his abuse of fashion. White kid gloves on the hands of a conductor he scoffed at. 'Who can do anything fettered with these things?' he pettishly insisted; and it was only after considerable pressure and pointing out the aristocratic antecedents of the Philharmonic and the class of its supporters that he had consented to wear a pair to walk up the steps of the orchestra on first appearing, to be taken off immediately he got to his desk. . . . What a pleasant impres- sion did the master give us by his childlike jollity. Full of fun, he exhibited his remarkable power of imitation. He was a born actor, and it was impossible not to recognise immediately who was the individual caricatured, for Wagner's power of observation led him at all times to notice the most minute characteristics of all whom he encountered. . . ."

The most interesting feature of Wagner's visit to London in 1855 was his meeting with Berlioz. The ordinary conductor of the New Philharmonic was a Dr. Wilde, "a typical chubby-faced Eng- lishman," says Wagner, "who had been trained by the Stuttgart conductor Lindpaintner "up to the point of at least attempting to catch up the

orchestra with his beat, the orchestra itself going
its own way entirely. I heard a Beethoven Symphony performed in this fashion and was surprised
to hear the audience break into precisely the same
applause with which it greeted one of my own
strictly accurate and really fiery performances.
To lend distinction to these concerts, however,
they had . . . invited Berlioz over for some of
them. I then heard him conduct some classical
works, such as a Mozart Symphony, and was
amazed to find a conductor who was so energetic
in the interpretation of his own compositions, sink
into the commonest rut of the vulgar time-beater.
Certain of his own compositions, such as the more
effective fragments from the "Romeo and Juliet"
symphony, again made a particular impression
on me, it is true; but I was now more consciously
awake to the curious weaknesses which disfigure
even the finest conceptions of this extraordinary
musician. . . .

"I felt much stimulated, however, on the two
or three occasions when Sainton invited me to
dine with Berlioz. I was now brought face to face
with this strangely gifted person, tormented and
even blunted in some respects as he then was.
When I saw him, a man considerably my senior,
coming here in the hope of earning a few guineas,
I could deem myself perfectly happy, and almost
floating on air by contrast; for my own coming
had been brought about rather by a desire for
distraction, a craving for outward inspiration.
His whole bearing expressed weariness and despair, and I was suddenly seized with sympathy
for this man, whose talent so far surpassed that
of his rivals – for this was clear as daylight to me.

Berlioz seemed to be pleasantly affected by the
attitude of gay spontaneity I adopted with him.
His usual short, almost reserved manner thawed
visibly during the friendly hours we passed
together. . . ."

It is pleasant to know on Praeger's authority
that Wagner's sympathy for Berlioz was genuine.
Of course it is quite clear that Wagner did not
understand Berlioz, but he could not be the artist
he was without having some instinctive sympathy
for another artist of such obvious genius. Praeger
relates how a musical amateur named Krauss,
who was in the confidence of the French Emperor
Napoleon III and held a position in his household,
came to London on a visit, and as he was an
admirer of Wagner, he was brought to see him.

"Now listen to what took place," says Praeger.
"Wagner did all that was possible by persuasive
language to induce Krauss to move the Emperor
to do something for Berlioz. It was to no purpose
that we were told the Emperor was not enthusiastic for music and that so many impossible
difficulties were in the way. Wagner kept to his
point; Berlioz was poor, had been compelled to
resort to pledging trinkets, etc., whereby to live,
and that it was a crime to the art which he,
Krauss, professed to love that Berlioz should be
in want. I have thought this incident worthy of
notice, as showing the good-will of Wagner for
a brother artist was stronger than the icy restraint
that existed between them when they met."

But this "icy restraint," which Wagner with
his usual optimism considered he overcame by
his "gay spontaneity," is enormously significant
to those who can perceive from their music the

fundamental difference in nature between these two men of genius. "Hector Berlioz," says Praeger, "was of an excitable temperament, too, but he could repress it. Not so Wagner. He presented a striking contrast to the polished, refined Frenchman, whose speech was almost classic, through his careful selection of words."

The difference between them may be summed up simply in the statement that Wagner was not capable of detachment whereas Berlioz was. Berlioz, we know, had a highly developed dramatic sense; his command of what was effective was as remarkable as Wagner's; his own autobiography and his other writings show what a keen sense for situation and character Berlioz had. But Berlioz could stand apart from his rôle as an actor. He assumed the pose and the histrionic attitude deliberately when he wanted to, whereas the more one studies Wagner the more one is forced to the conclusion that he was born in his part as Richard Wagner and that he never ceased to play the rôle until the day of his death. It is that which makes him so much more effective than Berlioz, in whom we find the normal dualism of the highly gifted artist. Wagner was free from this dualism, he had the singleness, the integrity which, as a rule, only the greatest of men have; but, whereas their integrity is something godlike and superhuman, the integrity of Wagner is something more primitive, something rather pre-godlike and subhuman.

If this seems unfair, let me quote the description by the enthusiastic Praeger of his idol:

"Who can picture the composer of that colossal work of intellect, the 'Nibelung-Ring,' sitting at

the piano, in an elegant, loose robe-de-chambre,
singing, with full heart, snatches and scenes from
his 'adored' idol Weber's *Euryanthe* and, at in-
tervals of every three or four minutes, indulging
in large quantities of scented snuff. The snuff-
taking of the evening is the deeper graven on my
memory, because Wagner abruptly stopped singing on finding his snuff-box empty and got into
a childish, pettish fit of anger. He turned to us in
deepest concern with 'kein Schnuff-tabac mehr
also kein Gesang mehr' (no more snuff, no more
song); and though we had reached the small
hours of early morn would have someone start in
search of this 'necessary adjunct.' "

The year following his London visit was spent at
Zurich, and Wagner continued working at *Siegfried*, as we have seen, until well into the year 1857,
although he began to be more and more pre-
occupied with the idea of composing an opera on
the subject of *Tristan* which might be easier to get
performed than his immense tetralogy. This
coincided with a greater intimacy with Otto and
Mathilde Wesendonck which had developed.
Otto Wesendonck had bought a large piece of
land on which to erect a new villa, and adjoining
this site was a charming little country house with
a garden. This Wesendonck bought and let to
Wagner at a nominal rental, and Wagner moved
into this house about Easter 1857. The Wesendoncks moved into their new villa about mid-
summer 1857, and now they were close neigh-
bours. Wagner's own account of the closer relationship, in his autobiography, is as follows:

"About this time the Wesendoncks moved into
their villa, which had now been embellished by

stucco-workers and upholsterers from Paris. At
this point a new phase began in my relations with
this family which was not really important but
nevertheless exercised considerable influence on
the outward conduct of my life. . . . I had often
noticed that Wesendonck, in his straightforward
open manner, had shown uneasiness at the way
in which I made myself at home in his house. In
many things, in the matter of heating and lighting
the rooms, and also in the hour appointed for
meals, consideration was shown me which seemed
to encroach upon his rights as master of the house.
It needed a few confidential discussions on the
subject to establish an agreement which was half
implied and half expressed. This understanding
had a tendency, as time wore on, to assume a
double significance in the eyes of other people
and necessitated a certain measure of precaution
in an intimacy which had now become exceedingly close. These precautions were occasionally
a source of great amusement to the two parties
who were in the secret. Curiously enough, this
closer association with my neighbour coincided
with the time when I began to work out my
libretto *Tristan und Isolde*."

This is an admirable example of Wagner's
ingenuity in describing important events in his
life without revealing their true significance. Beside this extract from his autobiography must be
placed the following passage which, Dr. Julius
Kapp states, was originally suppressed in the
published Wesendonck letters.

"Wesendonck," writes Wagner, "could not, in
the face of his wife's unconcealed candour, fail to
become increasingly jealous. Her greatness lay in

the fact that she kept her husband steadily informed of the state of her heart, bringing him
gradually to the point of giving her up entirely.
The sacrifices and struggles involved in this may
be imagined. That she succeeded was due solely
to the depth and nobility of her absolutely unselfish love; this gave her the strength to reveal
herself as a person of such significance that when
she finally threatened him with her death he had
to stand aside and prove his unshakable love for
her by supporting her even in her anxiety for me.
In the last resort he wished to keep the mother of
his children, and for their sakes – it was they who
separated us both most invincibly – he accepted
his renunciatory position. Thus, while he was
consumed with jealousy, she was still able to
interest him in me to the extent of frequently
subsidising me. When at last it was a question
of my wish to have a little house and garden, it
was she who, by the most incredible battles, persuaded him to buy for me the fine piece of land
beside his own. Most marvellous of all, I had
practically never a suspicion of all this fighting.
Her-husband had to maintain a perfectly friendly,
natural manner with me on her account. There
must be no gloomy looks to reveal the situation to
me, no ruffling of a single hair of my head. Even
the sky above me was to be serene and cloudless,
and the ground soft to my tread. Such was the
incredible triumph of this noblest of women's
glorious love."

Those who have an ear for prose will be struck
by the extraordinary similarity between Wagner's
writing and his music. In both, we meet with his
"idealism" in full blast, and this "idealism" is

H

as astonishing in its richness and elaboration as it
is unconvincing. The intimacy between Wagner
and Mathilde Wesendonck was the cause of the
most painful experiences for all four concerned.
Minna Wagner was naturally jealous and so was
Otto Wesendonck, and it is now clear, through
the publication of much correspondence that had
been suppressed or had remained unknown until
recent years, that a great deal of the trouble was
caused by the tactless behaviour of both Mathilde
Wesendonck and Wagner. There were frequent
crises between September 1857 and August 1858.
In a letter of September 1857 Minna writes: "I
really had to give Frau Wesendonck a piece of
my mind, she behaved in such a haughty and
idiotic way to me all at once that I refused her
invitations. But she afterwards begged my par-
don, and now I am friends with her again for
Richard's sake."

The situation was exceptionally difficult owing
to the proximity in which the two families lived
and became so strained that at the beginning of
1858 Wagner made a trip to Paris. In Paris he
called on Ollivier, who had married Liszt's daughter, Blandine; also he heard Berlioz read to him
the libretto for his new opera *The Trojans*. He
comments on the latter incident with all the noble
magnanimity of an actor: "In order to get an
impression of the work I was particularly anxious
to hear the libretto Berlioz had written himself,
and he spent an evening reading it out to me.
I was disappointed in it, not only as far as it was
concerned, but also by his singularly dry and
theatrical delivery. I fancied that in the latter
I could see the character of the music to which

he had set his words, and I sank into utter despair about it, as I could see that he regarded this as his masterpiece and was looking forward to its production as the great object of his life."

On his return to Zurich the tension increased and finally came to a crisis through Minna's opening a packet and a letter sent by Wagner to Mathilde. This packet contained sketches of the music to the first act of *Tristan*, and the love letter disturbed Minna to such an extent that she had an interview with Mathilde. Minna imagined that she was thereby averting a calamity, but actually, of course, she merely precipitated one. Minna wrote at the time:

"Frau Wesendonck was really most grateful and friendly . . . and we parted in agreement and on good terms. But behind my back she seems to have changed her mind. She told her husband that I had offended her dreadfully, without, however, telling him the plain truth about what had been going on. To Richard she actually made a hullabaloo about the deep and dreadful way I had insulted her, although I had the delicacy not even to show this woman the compromising letter in my pocket. But that is the way with these mean vulgar natures, they can do nothing but tell tales and bait people."

Wesendonck took his wife away to Italy for a tour, and Minna went to Brestenberg for a cure for heart trouble. When they all had returned a succession of guests prevented any further conflict for a time; among these guests were Hans von Bülow and his wife Cosima, Liszt's daughter. The final rupture came, however, and is best described in a letter from Minna to a friend, dated August 2nd, 1858, from which I take the following:

"On the point of leniency towards men I am just as enlightened as any other woman and have overlooked many things, preferring not to notice them. After all, for six whole years I ran blindly alongside. Now Richard's honour simply won't allow him to stay here, as the husband has become aware of the affair, I don't know how. When I came back, my husband was so violent in his demand that I should return to the old footing with that woman, that I gave way and made this gigantic effort. It is really the utmost that a woman could do in my place. However, the husband, and, in the end, this woman will not have it so. She is furious – my husband shouted the fact to me himself – and is beside herself with fury at my being here, her jealousy will not allow me to remain; only Richard is to live here – which of course he cannot do. Richard has two hearts: one side of him is entangled, while from force of habit he is still attached to me – that is all. As this woman will not let me stay with my husband, and as he is weak enough to do her will, I have decided to stay alternately in Dresden, Berlin and Weimar until it shall please Richard or God to call me. My health is naturally no better in these conditions, not all the spas in the world can do anything in the face of these emotional storms. . . . In a fortnight, as soon as the visitors have gone – I mean to keep them as long as possible – I shall have to get busy with selling and packing the furniture. Richard will be going off beforehand, I do not know where; perhaps to Italy. I never speak to him about this affair. We are to all appearance on good terms. He suffers sometimes, though not on my account – while I suffer only on his. I hate the world, where all these weak people torment each other."

On August 17th, 1858, Wagner left his little house, "Asyl," for Venice, and Minna went to Dresden. The stimulus of his feelings for Mathilde Wesendonck and the enforced separation, from which it is clear he suffered, drove him to concentrate on continuing the composition of *Tristan*. He completed the second act at Venice during the winter of 1858, and moved to Lucerne in March 1859. Meanwhile Minna had busied herself at Dresden in trying to get the ban on Wagner's return to Germany removed, but without immediate success. From Lucerne Wagner paid several visits to the Wesendoncks, and says: "I spent some days in my friends' house, where I saw my old Zurich acquaintances again and felt as though I was passing from one dream to another. In fact everything assumed an air of unsubstantiality for me." He says that the months of April, May and the greater part of June passed without his finishing even half the third act of *Tristan*, and that all the time he was in a mood of the deepest melancholy. By the end of August, however, he had made considerable progress and was in a milder mood. He and Minna had constantly corresponded, although they had now been separated for about a year. As he could not yet obtain an amnesty enabling him to return to Germany, he decided to go to Paris and arranged that Minna should join him there. On September 7th, 1859, he left for a three days' visit to the Wesendoncks and made Wesendonck an offer that he should

buy the copyright of the *Nibelungen*. "Wesendonck," he says, "acceded to my wishes without
demur and was ready to buy out each of the completed portions of my work in turn for about the
same sum as it was reasonable to suppose a
publisher would pay for it later on."

Furnished with funds, Wagner reached Paris
on September 15th. He took a house in the Rue
Newton, and Minna arrived on November 17th.
He heard that the publisher Schott, of Mayence,
was anxious to secure a new opera by him, and
Wagner succeeded in selling him *Rheingold* for ten
thousand francs, giving him the option of pur-
chasing the remaining three operas of the "Ring"
for the same amount each. He then made preparations for giving some concerts of his own music
in Paris. The first took place on January 25th,
the second on February 1st and the third on
February 8th, 1860. They were a great success
artistically, and the audiences were enthusiastic,
but there was a loss of about five thousand francs
on the first concert and a somewhat smaller loss
on the other two. These concerts, however, increased Wagner's reputation considerably and
won him many new friends, of whom the most
notable was the poet Baudelaire, who wrote about
his music and became his most ardent champion
in Paris. Of Baudelaire Wagner writes: "his
opinions . . . which he expressed in the most
fantastic terms and with audacious self-assurance
proved him, to say the least, a man of extraordinary understanding, who with impetuous
energy followed the impressions he received from
my music to their ultimate consequences."

Wagner now concentrated upon obtaining the

use of the Imperial Opera House in Paris. His
young friend, Hans von Bülow, came with an introduction from the Princess-Regent of Prussia to
the Ambassador, Count Portales, and, through
von Bülow, Count Portales and Count Paul Hatz-
felt became very friendly to Wagner. It was,
however, through Princess Metternich that the
Emperor, Napoleon III, suddenly ordered that
Tannhäuser should be performed at the Opera
House. In the meantime Wagner had spent all
his money and was in desperate straits, but was
temporarily relieved by a loan of three thousand
francs from a Mme Schwabe and a gift of ten
thousand francs from Frau Marie Kalergis.
Wagner was growing more and more hardened,
his best creative period was largely over, and he
concentrated more and more upon obtaining
public recognition and money. We get a vivid
glimpse of his life in Paris at this time from a letter
written by Minna, on March 24th, 1860, to Emma
Herwegh:

"On Wednesday our little drawing-room is
open to acquaintances and friends, and we have
a lot of people. Except on these occasions, I do
not see anyone here whom I like. Blandine is
quite a common – I will not say low – person.
Her reputation is not good with anyone who
knows her – though that does not mean much in
Paris. Narrow-minded people, among whom
I fear I must count myself, find her almost
repugnant. Frau Ollivier (Blandine) often comes
to see my husband without having the decency
to ask for me. I am used to that kind of thing
and let everything happen without taking the least
notice . . . my husband is entirely uninterested

in anything that concerns me . . . when I received your last letter, asking for two tickets for M. and Mme Challemel, I handed Richard the page, turned down, as I have several times asked in vain for a couple of concert tickets when I could not help hearing that Frau Blandine had whole boxes almost pressed upon her to choose from. Hans von Bülow has been here nearly two months and has given four concerts during that time, which were well attended by very enthusiastic audiences. You will have met his wife, Cosima, in Berlin. She is another rather fast creature. It is her fault that Ritter left his wife – the poor young thing is pining away. Bülow looks perfectly wretched, we often had him to dinner. . . ."

Dr. Julius Kapp states: "The *liaison* between Wagner and Liszt's eldest daughter, Blandine, to which Minna alluded, had aroused much comment in Paris. Blandine was the wife of the advocate, Ollivier, who later became Minister of Justice. It was this affair that was at the root of Princess Wittgenstein's definite break with Wagner at that time and of her failure to make any contact with him in Paris in 1860. (In the Wagner literature not a word has been breathed about this association, the omission being the easier for the fact that all the passages relating to it were eradicated from the published Wagner letters. Later publications will have much interesting material to bring forward.)"

Meanwhile the preparations for the production of *Tannhäuser* went on. In July of 1860 Minna went for a cure to the baths of Soden near Frankfurt, and about this time, owing to the intervention of powerful friends, King John of Saxony agreed to raise no objection to Wagner's being admitted to any German state except his own, Saxony. Consquently Wagner was able to set foot on German soil for the first time since his flight from Dresden in 1849; so in August 1860 he met Minna at Soden, and went with her to Baden-Baden, and ultimately returned to Paris after a trip on the Rhine from Mannheim to Cologne. On his way he met a young banker, Emil Erlanger, who offered him financial assistance which Wagner, as usual, was happy to accept. In the winter of 1860 Wagner re-wrote part of *Tannhäuser* and superintended the rehearsals. He was severely ill in November and December, but the rehearsals were continued in the new year and the famous first performance of *Tannhäuser* in Paris took place on March 13th, 1861. The second performance was on March 18th, and after the third performance the opera was withdrawn at Wagner's request. The fiasco of *Tannhäuser* was due to the hostility of a clique, the members of the Jockey Club, who were the cause of extraordinary scenes in the theatre. Wagner was now again without funds or prospects, but he was helped once more by a Herr Stürmer and by Princess Metternich and Count Hatzfeld, who raised a considerable sum of money for him. Furnished with a Prussian passport, Wagner left Paris in August 1861 and returned to Germany, having spent twelve years in exile.

CHAPTER VI

1861–1883

It was now arranged that Minna should settle in Dresden, where she had friends, and that Wagner should look about him in Germany for "a new centre of operations." Wagner then went to Weimar, where he enjoyed himself with Liszt, the Olliviers and Bülow. After Bülow's departure a day before the others, Wagner relates that he said to Liszt: "There was no necessity for him to marry Cosima," and that Liszt replied: "That was a luxury." Wagner then went to Vienna, where there was the possibility of getting *Tristan* produced at the Imperial Opera House. Difficulties with singers seemed insuperable, and in September he accepted an invitation from the Wesendoncks to meet them in Venice. He says: "They seemed to have no desire to realise my position in Vienna. Indeed, after the ill-success of my Paris undertaking entered upon with such glorious anticipations, I had learned to recognise among most of my friends a tacitly submissive abandonment of all hope for my future success."

It was during this trip to Venice that the idea of the *Meistersinger* came into Wagner's mind; due partly, it appears, to the fact that it became clear that Mathilde and Otto Wesendonck were completely reconciled and that she could be now no more than a friend. When he returned to Vienna he studied Grimm and also Wagenseil's *Nuremburg Chronicle* at the Imperial Library. In order to obtain some means of livelihood while writing and composing a new work, Wagner negotiated with the publisher Schott and obtained an advance of three thousand marks. He succeeded, however, in getting more money from Schott, and about the middle of December started for Paris and stayed at the Hôtel Voltaire, where he finished the libretto of the *Meistersinger* by the end of January 1862. He then left for Biebrich, on the Rhine, where Minna came and stayed for about a week before returning to Dresden. Wagner made friends with Friederike Meyer, a pretty young actress playing in Frankfurt, and with another young woman, Mathilde Maier, who was also very helpful to him. In the summer of 1862 he resumed work:

"As from the balcony of my flat, in a sunset of great splendour, I gazed upon the magnificent spectacle of 'golden' Mayence with the majestic Rhine flowing along its outskirts in a glory of light, the prelude to my *Meistersinger* again suddenly made its presence clearly and distinctly felt on my soul. Once before I had seen it rise before

me out of a lake of sorrow, like some distant
mirage. I proceeded to write down the prelude
exactly as it appears to-day in the score, that is,
containing the clear outlines of the leading themes
of the whole drama. I proceeded at once to con-
tinue the composition, intending to allow the
remaining scenes to follow in due succession."

In July 1862 Hans von Bülow and his wife
Cosima paid a visit to Wagner at Biebrich, and
to them and other friends he read the libretto
of the *Meistersinger* and with Bülow's assistance
played the portions of the music that had been
composed. The marriage of Hans von Bülow
and Cosima Liszt seems to have been largely a
marriage of ambition on the part of Cosima, who
was passionately interested in her husband's career
as a musician and was always urging him to
creative work, even herself writing librettos for
him to compose music to. It became clear that
Bülow had no real creative power, and contact
with Wagner made him more keenly aware of his
own limitations. Bülow himself wrote: "With
Wagner as one's neighbour everything shrinks so
wretchedly to nothing and becomes childish,
empty and futile . . . I wish it were time to fall
asleep and have it all over. I have lost all my
self-assurance and with it all desire to live. What
can one do with just feeble piety?"

Wagner, writing of their visit to Biebrich and
the final excursion they took together, says:

"This time we could take leave of one another
cheerfully, although the increasing and often
excessive ill-humour of poor Hans had drawn
many an involuntary sigh from me. He seemed
to be in perpetual torment. On the other hand,

Cosima appeared to have lost the shyness she had evinced towards me . . . and a very friendly manner had taken its place. While I was singing 'Wotan's Abschied' to my friends, I noticed the same expression on Cosima's face as I had seen on it, to my astonishment, in Zurich on a similar occasion, only the ecstasy of it was transfigured into something higher. Everything connected with this was shrouded in silence and mystery, but the belief that she belonged to me grew to such certainty in my mind, that when I was under the influence of more than ordinary excitement my conduct betrayed the most reckless gaiety. As I was accompanying Cosima to the hotel across a public square, I suddenly suggested she should sit in an empty wheelbarrow which stood in the street so that I might wheel her to the hotel. She assented in an instant. My astonishment was so great that I felt all my courage desert me and was unable to carry out my mad project."

The Bülows returned to Berlin, and Wagner soon went to Vienna, where there was a renewed prospect of getting *Tristan* performed. On his way he gave a concert on November 1st, 1862, at the Leipzig Gewandhaus, where he conducted the first performance of the *Meistersinger* overture. The well-known writer Eduard Dannreuther has given an account of this concert in Grove's Dictionary in which he says:

"The writer, who was present, distinctly remembers the half-empty room, the almost complete absence of professional musicians, the wonderful performance and the enthusiastic demand for a repetition, in which the members of the orchestra took part as much as the audience."

Wagner then paid a visit to Minna in Dresden (the ban on his entry to Saxony having been lifted, after incessant application, that year). He stayed some days with her in the flat she had prepared for him, and then left to return to Biebrich before going to Vienna. This was the last occasion on which he and Minna were to meet. He says:

"After I had provided Minna with enough money to last some time, she accompanied me back to the station on the fourth day, but she was filled with such fearful presentiments of never seeing me again that her farewell was made in positive anguish."

In the meantime Cosima von Bülow had obtained, through her father, Liszt, "a considerable sum" of money for Wagner from the Grand Duke of Weimar, and on November 15th, 1862, Wagner left Biebrich for Vienna, accompanied by Friederike Meyer. Peter Cornelius, the composer of the comic opera *Der Barbier von Bagdad*, who was one of the many young musicians who attached themselves to Wagner, was in Vienna and wrote at the time the following account of Wagner:

"We have been to see Wagner. He was giving a musical evening for his Fräulein Friederike Meyer. Her maid sat in the room to chaperon her. This business with Friederike is not so bad as they made out in Mainz. She is quite a nice girl – as far as one can see – intelligent without trying to impress anyone with the fact; not particularly pretty, but had a lively expression. Wagner behaves very prettily and decently in her presence. If he absolutely must have some *liaison*, this one seems to suit him very tolerably."

The projected performance of *Tristan* in Vienna
fell through, but Wagner arranged a series of three
concerts between January 1st and January 8th,
1863, at which selections from *Rheingold, Walküre,
Siegfried* and *Meistersinger* were performed to increasing audiences. There was, however, a heavy
financial loss which was met by money obtained
through the intermediary of his friends, chiefly
Mme Kalergis, who had succeeded in getting the
young Empress Elizabeth to attend one of the
concerts. It was partly through Mme Kalergis
that Wagner now received an invitation to conduct two concerts in St. Petersburg for the Philharmonic Society, for a fee of two thousand silver
roubles. On the way, he gave a concert in Prague,
which brought him in two thousand marks. In
St. Petersburg his music made a great impression.
The audiences were wildly enthusiastic, and the
orchestra of one hundred and twenty musicians
equally so; "from some of them," relates
Wagner, "I heard such exclamations as, 'we
must admit we have never known what music is
till now.'" It is characteristic of Wagner that,
in spite of the enormous success of his two official
concerts and the profitable results of his own concert in the Imperial Opera House, he complains
of having to give a fourth concert, the proceeds
of which were to go to the conductor, Schuberth,
who had assisted him: "So a week later," he
says, "I repeated the most popular items of my
programme before an equally numerous audience
and with the same success, but this time the handsome receipts of three thousand roubles were
destined for an invalid man, who, as a retribu-
tion for this encroachment on my rights, was

suddenly summoned to another world in the same year."

In St. Petersburg he had friendly relations with Serov and Anton Rubinstein, and in Moscow with Nicholas Rubinstein; but his efforts to find financial support for the rest of his life were unavailing. He complains that a Prince Odoiewsky, to whom he had an introduction from Mme Kalergis, upon his having attempted "to give the genial Prince some idea of my position and my aspirations, with apparent emotion exclaimed: 'J'ai ce qu'il vous faut; parlez à Wolffsohn' "; but when Wagner enquired who Wolffsohn was he learned that "the guardian spirit thus commended to me was not a banker but a Russian Jew who wrote romances."

In April 1863, Wagner left Russia for Berlin, where he found Cosima in good health, having been delivered of her daughter Blandine a short time before. He spent some time with the Bülows in good spirits, having twelve thousand marks in cash after paying all expenses of his Russian trip and sending a thousand roubles to Minna. He decided that he would settle in Vienna and try to get *Tristan* performed there. He took a house at Penzing and moved into it on May 12th, and celebrated his fiftieth birthday there on May 22nd.

There are interesting details extant of his method of furnishing his Penzing villa. Dr. Julius Kapp states: "This reveller in silk and velvet was always changing his mind as new colour combinations occurred to him." He had two different upholsterers and a dressmaker, Bertha Goldwag, working for him, and Wagner's letters to this dressmaker have recently been published.

The general character of Wagner's taste in these
matters may be summed up in Dr. Kapp's own
words: "His personal wardrobe was also en-
trusted to Bertha. Coloured satin trousers with
jackets to match and slippers of the same shade,
everything being lined with wadding and fur,
were provided by her diligent fingers; also
twenty-four silk dressing-gowns of different
colours." Wagner's study had unusually soft and
heavy carpets, expensive cushions and rugs, and
the walls were hung with silk. It is possible to
make too much of all these luxuries, but the in-
terior of Wagner's Penzing house would certainly
have suggested that its occupier was a prima
donna rather than a creative artist. The fact that
Wagner suffered most of his life from erysipelas
must not be overlooked, for this made his skin
unusually sensitive, and silk, fur and wadding
had become indispensable to him.

The proceeds from his Russian tour were soon
spent, and Wagner's financial situation gradually
worsened. One cannot but sympathise with his
desperate need for money in order to be free to
compose: "My destiny is solitude, and my life
is work," he wrote on June 20th, 1863, to Nathalie,
with his usual gift for phrase-making. Actually
no musician ever had more friends or was less
solitary than Wagner, but the trouble was that he
needed a large degree of ease, luxury and leisure,
and this need became greater as he became older.
The amount of money he received through friends
and acquaintances is really astonishing, and, as
one example of Wagner's methods of extracting
money, I will quote two letters to Hornstein
written from 19 Quai Voltaire in Paris, where

I

he went to write the *Meistersinger* in 1861. The first is dated December 12th and is as follows:

"DEAR HORNSTEIN, – I hear that you have become rich. In what a wretched state I myself am you can easily guess from my failures. I am trying to retrieve myself by seclusion and a new work. In order to make possible this way to my preservation – that is to say, to lift me above the most distressing obligations, cares and needs that rob me of all freedom of mind – I require an immediate loan of ten thousand francs. With this I can again put my life in order and again do productive work. It will be rather hard for you to provide me with this sum; but it will be possible if you *wish* it and do not shrink from a sacrifice. This, however, I desire, and I ask it of you against my promise to endeavour to repay you in three years out of my receipts.

"Now let me see whether you are the right sort of man! If you prove to be such for me – and why should not this be expected of some-one some day? – the assistance you give me will bring you into very close touch with me, and next summer you must be pleased to let me come to you for three months at one of your estates, preferably in the Rhine district.

"I will say no more just now. Only, as regards the proposed loan, I may say that it would be a great relief to me if you could place even six thousand francs at my disposal immediately; I hope then to be able to arrange to do without the other four thousand francs until March. But nothing but the immediate provision of the whole sum can give me the

help which I so need in my present state of
mind. Let us see, then, and hope that the sun
will for once shine a little on me. What I need
now is a success; otherwise – I can probably
do nothing more!

"Yours,
"RICHARD WAGNER."

To this letter Hornstein sent a courteous reply
expressing his inability to do what Wagner asked;
privately he said that the fact that he knew he had
to deal with a "bottomless cask" and that Wagner
had bled numbers of people for large sums, made
his refusal easier. However, Wagner was more
than equal to Hornstein, and his reply is, in its
way, one of the best things Wagner ever wrote;
much better in my opinion than his essays into
philosophy and æsthetics:

"Paris, *December* 27th, 1861.

"DEAR HERR VON HORNSTEIN, – It would be
wrong of me to pass over without censure an
answer such as you have given me. Though
it will probably not happen again that a man
like me ("ein Mann meines Gleichen") will
apply to you, yet a perception of the impropriety
of your letter ought of itself to be a good thing
for you. You should not have presumed to
advise me in any way, even as to who is really
rich; and you should have left it to myself to
decide why I do not apply to the patrons and
patronesses to whom you refer. If you are not
prepared to have me at one of your estates, you
could have seized the signal opportunity I

offered you of making the necessary arrangements for receiving me in some place of my choice. It is consequently offensive of you to say that you will let me know when you will be prepared to have me. You should have omitted the wish you express with regard to my *Tristan*; your answer could only pass muster on the assumption that you are totally ignorant of my works. Let this end the matter. I reckon on your discretion, as you can on mine.

"Yours obediently,
"RICHARD WAGNER."

It is possible for us, in the light of subsequent events, to reflect that, if Wagner had not been able to borrow money all through his life, we should never have had the pleasure of hearing the "Ring," *Tristan und Isolde*, *Meistersinger*, and *Parsifal*. These operas have, since they were written, earned enormously more money than Wagner's total expenditure during his whole life – to say nothing of the pleasure, delight and stimulation they have given to hundreds of thousands of people. From a purely financial point of view, Wagner only received a small instalment of what he earned.

The only way left of getting any money was to give a concert tour, which he did in November 1863, staying in Berlin again with the Bülows. This apparently was the deciding meeting. The concerts were not very productive, one of the principal receipts being a gold snuff-box presented to Wagner by the Grand Duke of Baden for his second Karlsruhe concert, which he sold in Berlin for two hundred and seventy marks. "The

sum . . . was brought to me at the Hôtel Branden-
burg, where I was dining with the Bülows, and
was an addition to my reserves that furnished me
with many a jest. As Bülow had to complete the
preparations for his concert, I drove alone with
Cosima on the promenade, as before, in a fine
carriage. This time all our jocularity died away
into silence. We gazed speechless into each other's
eyes; an intense longing for an avowal of the
truth mastered us and led to a confession – which
needed no words – of the boundless unhappiness
which oppressed us. The experience brought
relief to us both, and the profound tranquillity
which ensued enabled us to attend the concert in
a cheerful unburdened mood."

Leaving Berlin, Wagner gave a concert for the
Prince of Hohenzollern-Hechingen, conducting
the Prince's private orchestra, and received a
generous fee of four thousand two hundred marks
which enabled him to send money to Minna and
pay a few urgent debts. This was his last piece
of good fortune for the time being. He spent
Christmas in Vienna and became ill in the New
Year of 1864. Being now completely without
money or prospects of getting any money, he says:
"The only course open to me was to see about
raising money by fresh bills at short dates, where-
with to pay all my other bills which were also
short-dated. Thus I became launched upon a
business system which, leading as it did to the
obvious and inevitable ruin, could only be finally
resolved by the acceptance of prompt and effectual
help."

By the end of February 1864 Wagner's position
had become desperate:

"My position was for some weeks most uncertain, until at last, it became clear that all my friends could procure me was the means of flight to Switzerland – which was now deemed absolutely necessary – where, having saved my skin so far, I shall have to raise money for my bills."

Accordingly, he left for Munich on March 23rd, and on the Good Friday, as he walked along the streets, he noticed the population in deep mourning for their King, Maximilian II, who had died a few days before, leaving as heir to the throne his son aged eighteen and a half. Wagner says: "I saw a portrait of the young king, Ludwig II, in a shop window and experienced the peculiar emotion which is aroused by the sight of youth and beauty placed in a position presumed to be unusually trying."

Arriving in Switzerland, Wagner found refuge in the house of Dr. Wille at Zurich, to whose wife he had written asking if she could put him up for a few days, after he had had a refusal from Otto Wesendonck to a similar request. On April 30th, Dr. Wille having returned from his absence in Constantinople, Wagner left Zurich for Stuttgart, where the conductor, Karl Eckert, of the Royal Court Theatre, was friendly to him. At Eckert's, on the evening of May 3rd, when he was discussing his situation with his friends and wondering how he could get enough money to settle his bills and get a little peace to return to the composition of the first act of the *Meistersinger*, a gentleman's card with the inscription "Secretary to the King of Bavaria" was handed to him. He made an appointment with this gentleman for the next

morning at 10 o'clock. I will describe this extraordinary event in Wagner's own words:

"I received Herr Pfistermeister, the private
secretary of H.M. the King of Bavaria, in my
room. He first expressed great pleasure at having
found me at last, thanks to receiving some happy
directions after vainly seeking me in Vienna and
even at Mariafeld on Lake Zurich. He was
charged with a note for me from the King of
Bavaria, together with a portrait and a ring as
a present. In words which, though few, penetrated
to the very core of my being, the youthful monarch
confessed his great partiality for my work and
announced his firm resolve to keep me near him
as his friend, so that I might escape any malignant
stroke of fate. Herr Pfistermeister informed me
at the same time that he was instructed to conduct
me to Munich at once, to see the King, and begged
my permission to inform his master by telegram
that I would come on the following day."

There is something so Wagnerian about this
climax that it leaves one amazed at the mysterious-
ness of human life. After telling us that he left
for Munich with Herr Pfistermeister at 5 o'clock
that afternoon, Wagner ends his autobiography
with the following words:

"On the same day I had received the most
urgent warnings against returning to Vienna.
But my life was to have no more of these alarms;
the dangerous road along which fate beckoned me
to such great ends was not destined to be clear of
troubles and anxieties of a kind unknown to me
heretofore, but I was never again to feel the weight
of the everyday hardships of existence under the
protection of my exalted friend."

In April, Wagner returned to Vienna with fifteen thousand gulden, to settle with his most pressing creditors, make arrangements with all the others, and get together what was left of his Penzing possessions. He returned with his servants, Anna and Franz Mrazek, to Munich and then, at the King's wish, went to a villa near the King's summer residence on Lake Starnberg. He wrote ecstatic letters to his friends about his friendship with the King. To Frau Moukhanoff, for example, he says:

"Every day brings something more unusual and beautiful. Heaven has sent him to me; it is through him that I still exist and create. It is he whom I love . . . never, never has history had anything so marvellously beautiful, profound and exquisite as the relation of my King to me. Perhaps it only *could* happen just to me! My art lives in this glorious youth as a visible moving force. He is my father, my country, my happiness."

Wagner was more than adequate to his new situation, as is shown in the style in which he writes: "Every day he (the King) sends for me once or twice, and I go on wings as if to my loved one. To know him like this is intoxicating. Never have I met so frank a thirst for knowledge, such comprehension, such a glow of response. Then this loving care of me, this charming purity of heart and of every look when he assures me how happy he is to have me! We often sit like this for hours, each lost in contemplation of the other."

Nevertheless, Wagner had other needs, and the most important was a woman to look after him and make a home for him. He writes to Frau

Wille that the deserted look of his house and the necessity for attending to everything himself cramped his spiritual life: "I have had to move again, furnish a house, give my mind to knives and forks, pots and pans, and bed-linen. I, the glorifier of women! And they leave me to do their jobs in this way! Shall I ever be able to 'renounce' women completely? The answer is no – with a big sigh – for I almost wish I could."

In the end Wagner wrote to the Bülows in June 1864, inviting Hans and Cosima "to come and stay with me this summer for as long as possible." He persisted and urged and cajoled until at last Bülow sent off Cosima and their two children (Daniela aged three and a half, and Blandine aged a year and three months) to Starnberg in advance of himself, being still detained by professional duties. This was the decisive step. Cosima, unknown to Hans, gave herself to Wagner and from that time Wagner and Cosima arranged matters to suit themselves. Wagner induced the King to make Hans von Bülow his court pianist, and it was arranged that the Bülows should come to Munich. The King provided Wagner with a magnificent villa in Munich, and, in November 1864 the Bülows arrived, and Cosima worked for several hours daily in Wagner's house, having a drawing-room and a study set apart for her. On April 10th, 1865, Cosima gave birth to a daughter of Wagner's, who was named Isolde. Bülow, whatever suspicions he may have had, accepted her, and Wagner was her godfather. The situation was extraordinary. There is a letter from Peter Cornelius to his fiancée about this time, in which he says:

"But the main thing is this love affair between Wagner and Cosima. . . . Since it began, Wagner has been entirely and unconditionally under her influence. With or without the two children she is with Wagner every day, now that Bülow is away on a concert tour. You can neither speak to him by himself nor write to him without having the letter opened and read to him by her. . . . And what is to become of Bülow? Has he really handed over his wife to Wagner on some highly romantic understanding? One must suppose that the marriage between Hans and Cosima has for some time past been a sham; otherwise Hans's behaviour would be inexplicable."

Wagner had kept in constant correspondence with Minna up to this time, but early in 1865 Minna made some reference to gossip she had heard, and Wagner sent her a reassuring telegram. On October 5th of the same year he wrote to her: "I have *not* read the letter just received from you. Ever since your letter last spring which so distressed me, I have been determined never again to allow anything to embitter my memory of you." In the meantime there was ever-growing hostility in Munich against Wagner on the part of those who were jealous of his position with King Ludwig. All who wanted something for themselves attacked him, and some of the newspapers even went so far in their attacks as to suggest that while he was living in splendour in Munich, Minna was starving in Dresden. Minna herself sent a public denial stating: "In connection with a rumour circulated by various Munich and Viennese papers I hereby state as a fact that I have up till now received from my absent husband Richard Wagner an allowance which guarantees me a care-free existence. It gives me great satisfaction to be able, by this explanation, to silence at least one of the many slanders that are brought against my husband."

Nevertheless, the attacks persisted and became so disturbing that at last the King requested Wagner to leave Munich temporarily, and so he went to Switzerland and then to Marseille, where he learnt the news of Minna's death on January 25th, 1866. In March, Cosima visited Wagner in Switzerland and they found an attractive house, "Triebschen," on the lake near Lucerne, and Wagner decided not to return to Munich. The King would have preferred to have Wagner nearer him, but he visited Wagner at Triebschen, where Wagner had invited Hans and Cosima to stay with him. Cosima arrived on May 12th, 1866. Wagner and Cosima continued to deceive the King, and the real situation was kept private, although public attacks were constantly being made on Wagner, Hans and Cosima; Wagner and Cosima actually got King Ludwig himself to attempt to silence the so-called slanders. The fall of Wagner's enemies from power in Bavaria changed the situation. It was possible for Wagner to return to Munich. The King made Hans von Bülow Court Conductor and gave him as a special honour the Cross of the Order of St. Michael. It was therefore necessary for Cosima and Hans to be together, and the Bülows took a flat in Munich in April 1867. Wagner's daughter Eva, born on February 17th, 1867, remained behind at Triebschen. Wagner came to Munich, stayed with the Bülows, and prepared for the famous first production of *Die Meistersinger*, which took place on June 21st, 1868, under von Bülow.

At the performance Wagner was in the royal box beside the King, and as a special favour the King signed to him to receive the applause from his privileged position. After this the storm burst. Wagner realised that it was impossible for him to remain in Munich and that he must retire to Triebschen, where he would need Cosima. Cosima joined him, and at last the true state of affairs became public and the King discovered that he had been completely deceived. It is said that the King never received Cosima again, not even in Bayreuth in 1876, but his friendship and support of Wagner continued.

From this time on Wagner led a life of comparative tranquillity. Cosima's marriage with Hans was annulled on July 18th, 1870. Cosima had become a Protestant, and married Wagner on August 25th, 1870, at Lucerne. At Triebschen, Wagner's son Siegfried was born, and there Wagner completed the "Ring." Here also it was that his friendship began with Nietzsche, then a young man of twenty-five, who was Professor of Philology at Basel University. Nietzsche was the last and perhaps the greatest of Wagner's conquests, and he helped Wagner in the propaganda for the building of a special festival theatre for the performances of Wagner's works. On May 22nd, 1872, Wagner's sixtieth birthday, the foundation of Bayreuth was laid, the money being raised partly by subscription, with the aid of innumerable Wagner societies. This event was celebrated by a special performance of Beethoven's Choral Symphony and Wagner moved his house for the last time from Triebschen, Lucerne, to Wahnfried, Bayreuth. In August 1876 the first performance of the completed "Der Ring des Nibelungen" took place at Bayreuth, but there was a deficit of £7,500, and it was to obtain money to wipe out this deficit that Wagner paid his third and last visit to London, in 1877, where he gave eight concerts at the Albert Hall. It was in London that he read to some of his friends the manuscript of *Parsifal* for the first time. He began the music to *Parsifal* in 1878 in his sixty-fifth year and completed it in April 1879, but the full scoring was not finished until January 1882. In July and August of 1882 the first performance of *Parsifal* was given at Bayreuth. After this production Wagner spent the winter in Venice, where he died of heart failure on February 13th, 1883, in his seventieth year.

It might truthfully be said, I believe, that Wagner was the most completely successful man who has ever lived. He achieved everything he set out to do. He completed, twenty-eight years after its first conception, the biggest work ever written for the stage, and saw it and all his other productions performed successfully in a special theatre of his own design built exclusively for him under his own superintendence at Bayreuth. For the last eighteen years of his life he dominated the musical world and lived in ease and luxury with his wife and children, having, apparently, every desire satisfied, seeing his fame growing greater and greater, and keeping the King of Bavaria as his friend and patron until the day of his death. He had completely triumphed over all his enemies and rivals. In the eyes of the world

there was no greater German living in 1882 than
Wagner, not even Bismarck; and to-day Bayreuth shares with Stratford-on-Avon the unique
distinction of having been made known all over
the world by the creative activity of a single
artist.

But even in his lifetime a small cloud had
appeared on the horizon; it was the defection
of his greatest disciple, Nietzsche. Nietzsche,
from being the most ardent and brilliant of the
Wagnerites, became, as early as 1876, doubtful
and then the bitterest and most hostile of the anti-
Wagnerites. Nietzsche wrote his famous *Der Fall
Wagner* ("The Case against Wagner") in 1888.
In this book we may find exposed the fundamental
weakness which has become more and more
apparent in Wagner's work. This weakness may
be described in Nietzsche's own words, when he
says that Wagner is always "swimming," never
"going." Or, it may be put in quite another
way. There is the reality of the visible world and
there is the reality of the invisible world, and in
the greatest works of art there is always a passage
or a "going" from one to the other. In Wagner
there is only a static reality, the reality of the set
stage and the puppet who has no connection with
any invisible reality. The stage is magnificent,
the puppets gorgeous, and the patron of the puppet show is the King of Bavaria. I would not
now say one word against that external magnifi-
cence which is not connected with the invisible
world. No doubt it has its place and its function
in the scheme of things, but: "Lay not up your
treasure upon the earth where the rust and moth
do corrupt and thieves break in and steal" means

that what is not connected with the invisible inevitably perishes. So we, in the twentieth century, are witnessing the gorgeous fabric of Wagner's music gradually crumbling into the dust.